Film Actresses

Volume 14

Norma Shearer

Documentary book

Part 1

ISBN-13 : 978-1502924858
ISBN-10 : 1502924854

Dtp
and
graphic design

Iacob Adrian

Author statement

The actors and actresses are the the bricks .

The cast and crew are the plaster .

They stand on the foundation created by
producers and writers and directors .

All these people creates the great palace
of the art of film .

Iacob Adrian - 2013

HOLLYWOOD

NRA

15c in Canada
10¢

February

NORMA SHEARER

Confessions of a
MOVIE PLAYGIRL

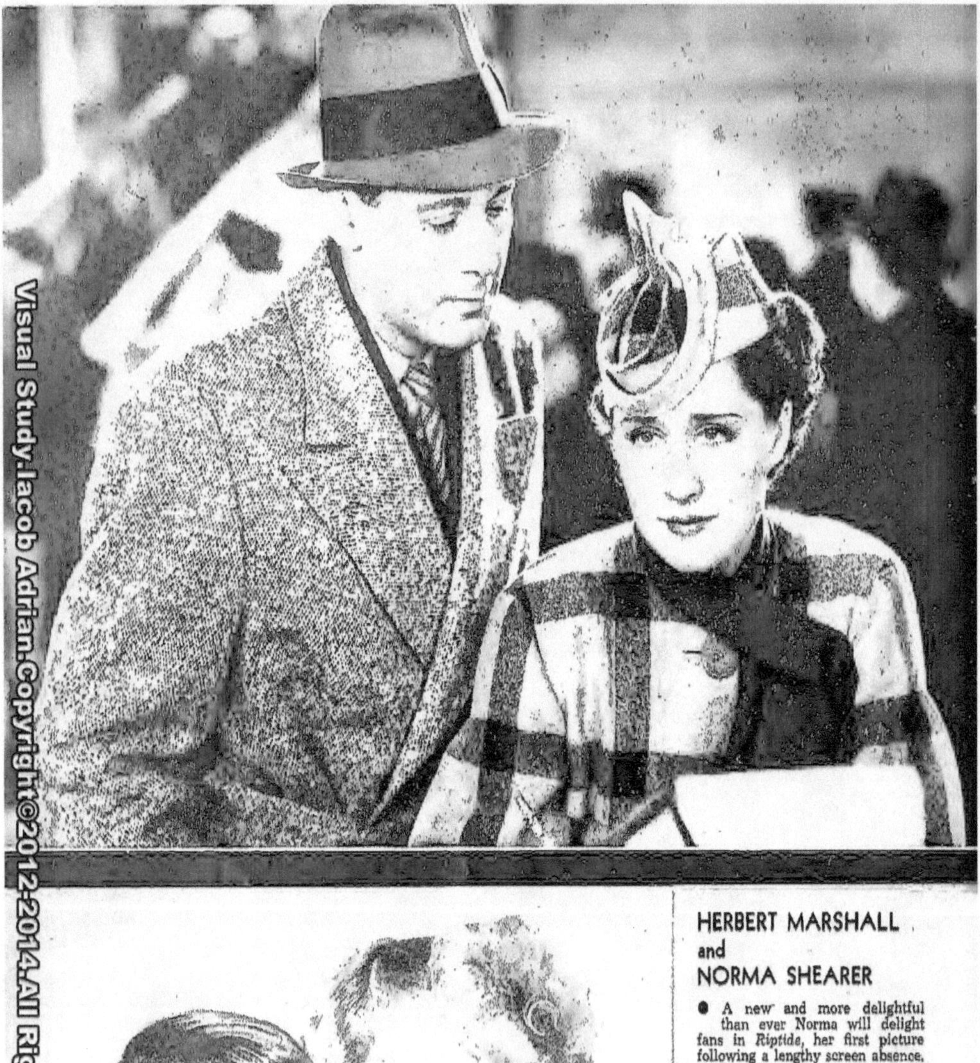

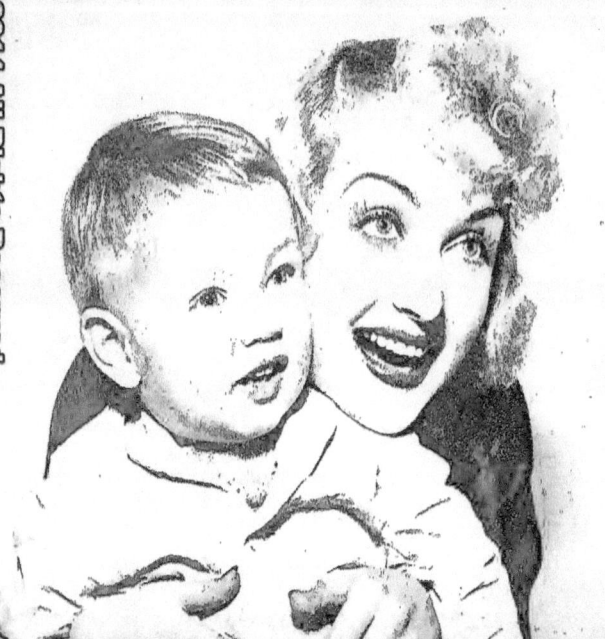

HERBERT MARSHALL
and
NORMA SHEARER

● A new and more delightful than ever Norma will delight fans in *Riptide*, her first picture following a lengthy screen absence. Herbert Marshall and Robert Montgomery share honors as her leading men

BABY LEROY
and
CAROLE LOMBARD

● Ah, *The Handsome Brute*— meaning Baby LeRoy, of course, who is slated for the picture of that title. Carole is now completing work in *We're Not Dressing* with Bing Crosby for Paramount

HOLLYWOOD

HOT FROM HOLLYWOOD...

Foreign Affairs

RICHARD DIX refused to sign a new contract with RKO-Radio because he wants to take an extended trip around the globe . . . Miriam Hopkins will go to the Argentine to do a picture for a South American concern . . . Beatrice Lillie's mate, Sir Robert Peel, died in England just as she prepared for a new try at American talkies . . . Germany banned *The Prizefighter and the Lady* because Max Baer is a Jew . . . Russians hail Charlie Chaplin as their idol because of his pro-Soviet views . . . the Benn Levys (Constance Cummings) will fly over France and Italy on their belated honeymoon . . . Maureen O'Sullivan is going to Ireland to bring back to Hollywood her twelve-year-old sister, Sheila . . . while abroad, Richard Arlen flew over those sections of England where he trained as an aviator during the World War. . . . Nils Asther has gone to Sweden to see his mother . . . Marlene Dietrich denies claims of Hitler's aides that she is a contributor to the Nazi treasury . . . the marriage of Pat Paterson, British-born, to Charles Boyer, a French subject, makes her French, too, so she's having a lot of worry over her passport . . . Burns and Allen, the nit-wits, are Europe-bound.

A sizzling pot-pourri of news

Stars Are on Guard

HOLLYWOOD ONCE AGAIN has taken on the appearance of an armed camp as a result of a new epidemic of extortion plots aimed at rich celluloid satellites.

Pistols that were stowed away a year ago when police roundups put an end to a long series of diamond robberies in Filmtown, now are being oiled up and reloaded, sharp-shooting bodyguards once more are in demand and other precautions taken by the silversheet's élite because of threats received by Mae West, Bing Crosby, Spencer Tracy, Loretta Young, Alice Brady, Ann Harding and Marian Nixon in recent weeks.

Katharine Pouts

KATHARINE HEPBURN, who dashed off to Paris for a three-day stay upon learning that she had been awarded the Academy statuette, is plenty miffed at her bosses in RKO-Radio.

Katie was offered $7,500 a week for a personal appearance tour on the strength of her artistic victory, but higher-ups quashed the idea under an iron heel.

They are banning all outside engagements for Hepburn — talkie and stage alike—until after she struts her stuff in their own *Joan of Arc*.

Marlene Super-Chef

MARLENE DIETRICH is unable to forget her domesticity even when she dines in a public place.

During Rudolph Sieber's recent visit to Hollywood, the German star took her husband and daughter, Maria, to the Russian Eagle for dinner. There General Lodijensky greeted her with a description of some new electrical equipment just installed in the culinary department.

"I'd like to see it," enthused Marlene.

The General led her off to the kitchen, where, following an exchange of toasts over a nip of vodka, Marlene donned an apron and supervised the preparation of the meal for Rudolph and Maria.

Mae's Bullet-Proof Car

MAE WEST is having an armored auto built by a Detroit manufacturer at a cost of $13,500. The heavy steel body is guaranteed to resist machine-gun fire.

Diamond Lil was marked for death by gangland when she brought about the arrest of two of the trio who robbed her of $17,000 in gems and cash eighteen months ago. One of the bandits, convicted on Mae's testimony, already is serving a prison term, while another is fighting extradition in Chicago.

Two husky detectives, assigned by District Attorney Buron Fitts, are constantly on guard over Mae.

Greta's Lonely Again!

IT'S ALL OVER between Greta Garbo and Rouben Mamoulian if you care to take the word of the chatterers.

Lending strength to the rumors that the Swede's newest romance has found its way into the refrigerator, however, is the fact that Greta once more is going places with her feminine pals.

Incidentally, the star has rescinded her demand on Metro that Mamoulian, who directed her in *Queen Christina*, be named to guide her through *The Painted Veil*, and has approved Richard Boleslavsky as her next megaphonist.

He Squires Marlene

AND as for Rouben, he doesn't care who sees him lunching with Marlene Dietrich at the Russian Eagle.

Connie Gives Up

CONSTANCE BENNETT apparently is through caring what the gossipers are saying about her friendship with Gilbert Roland. The pair are seen everywhere together.

Within a recent ten-day period the Los Angeles press recorded them as lunching at the Brown Derby, dining at the Russian Eagle, frolicking at Palm Springs, taking in the races at Caliente and—of all things!—attending services at the Beverly Hills Church of the Good Shepherd.

Norma Shearer swept to new heights of histrionic achievement in Riptide and is expected to continue her good work in The Barretts of Wimpole Street

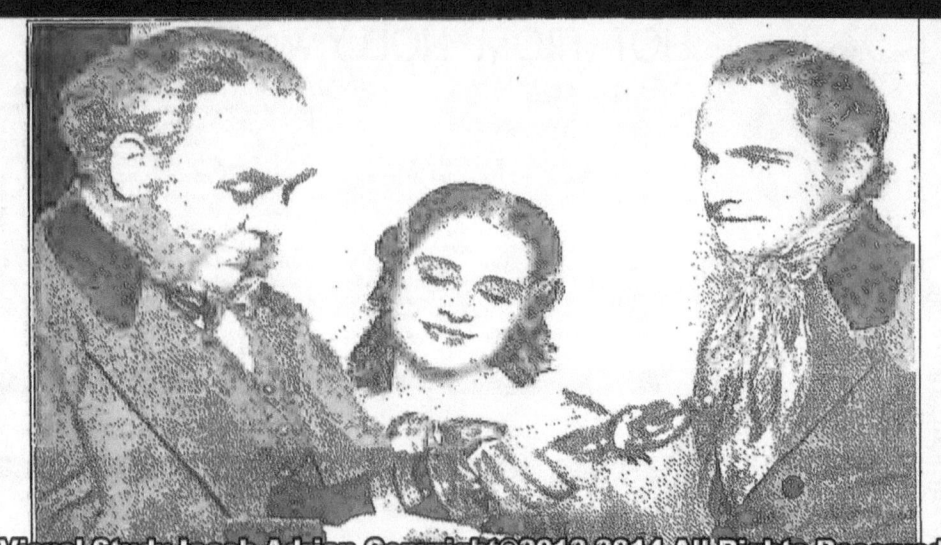

Charles Laughton admires the Academy award for the most outstanding screen performance of the year, while Norma Shearer and Fredric March, winners of the coveted prize in other years, look on

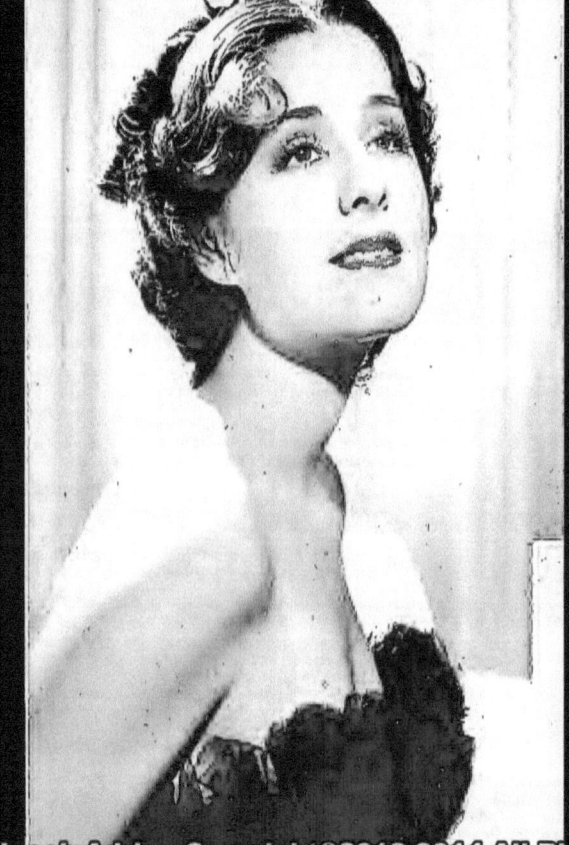

Right on the Set!

You're watching a scene of Norma Shearer's new picture being shot . . . so intimate you can almost touch Norma as she sits in her carriage

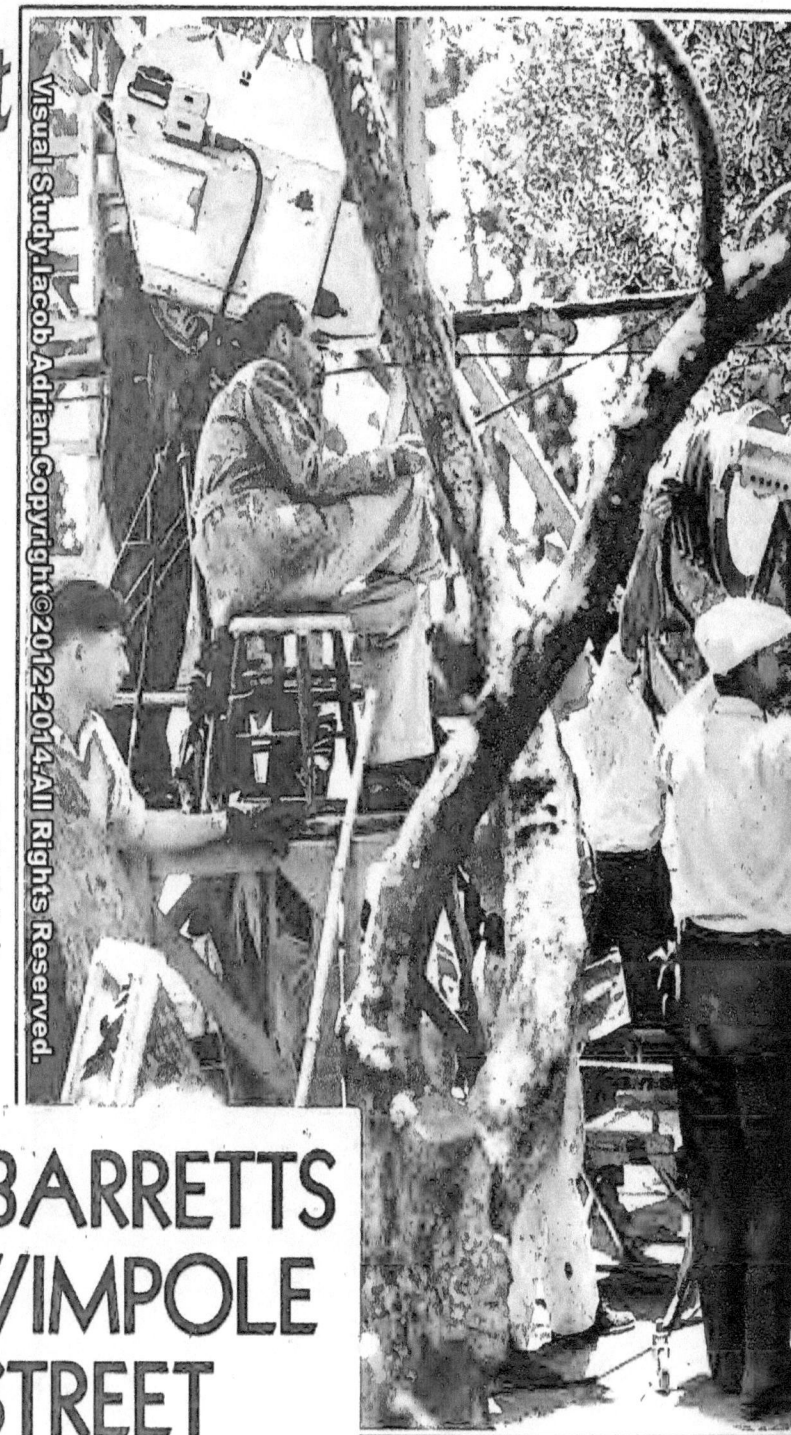

The BARRETTS of WIMPOLE STREET

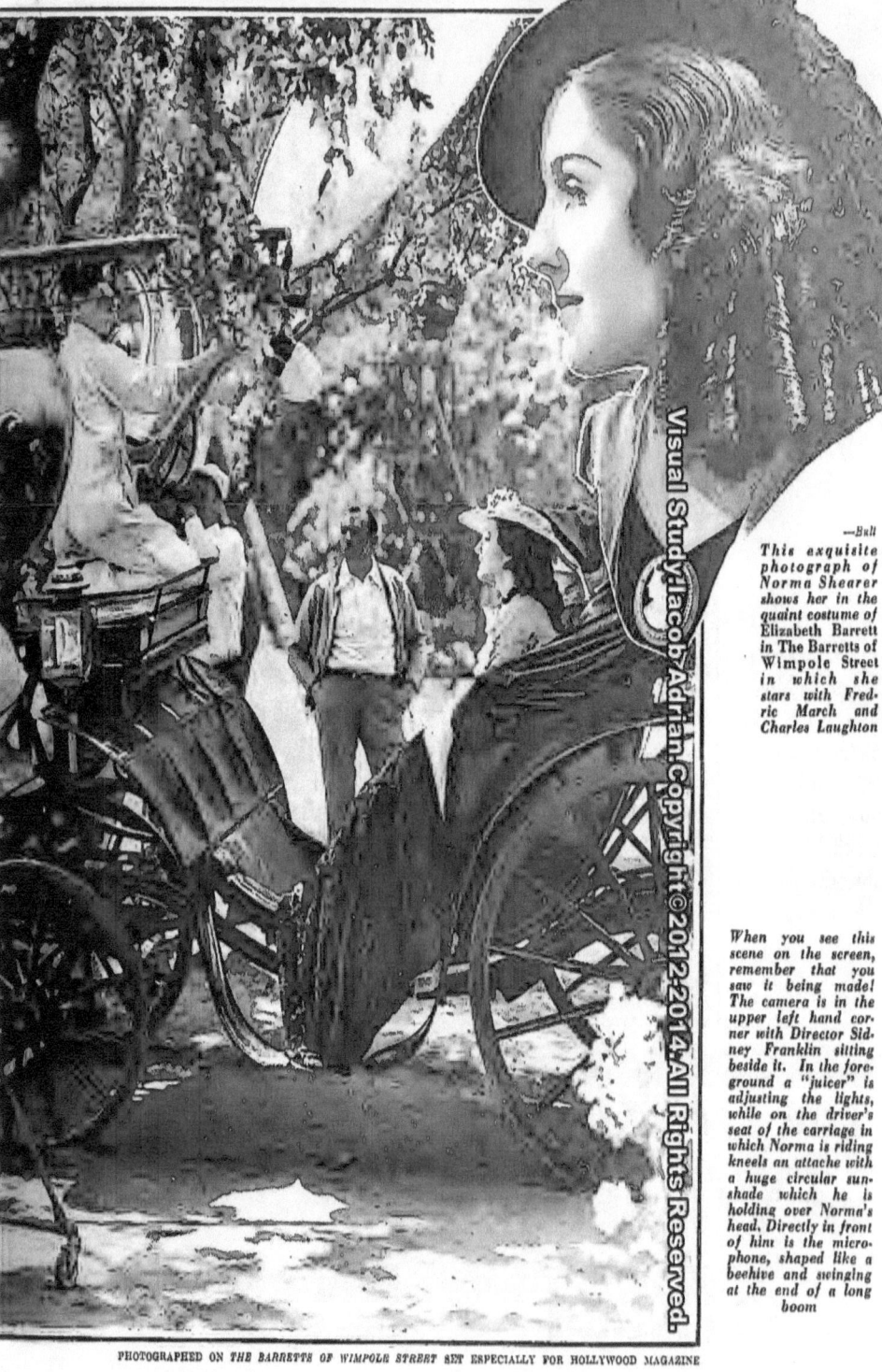

—Bull

This exquisite photograph of Norma Shearer shows her in the quaint costume of Elizabeth Barrett in The Barretts of Wimpole Street in which she stars with Fredric March and Charles Laughton

When you see this scene on the screen, remember that you saw it being made! The camera is in the upper left hand corner with Director Sidney Franklin sitting beside it. In the foreground a "juicer" is adjusting the lights, while on the driver's seat of the carriage in which Norma is riding kneels an attache with a huge circular sunshade which he is holding over Norma's head. Directly in front of him is the microphone, shaped like a beehive and swinging at the end of a long boom

PHOTOGRAPHED ON *THE BARRETTS OF WIMPOLE STREET* SET ESPECIALLY FOR HOLLYWOOD MAGAZINE

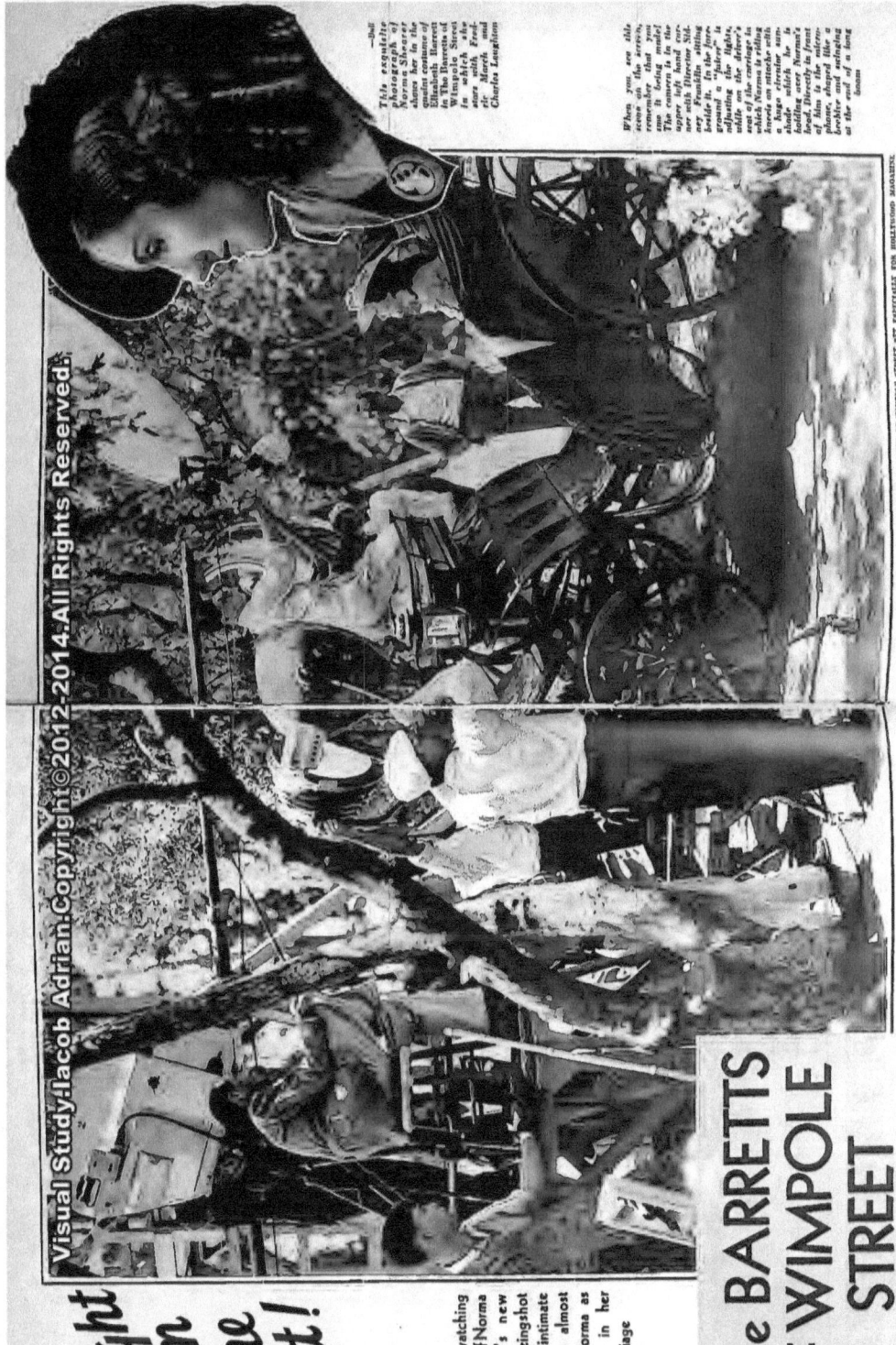

Right on the Set!

You're watching a scene of Norma Shearer's new picture being shot . . . so intimate you can almost touch Norma as she sits in her carriage

—*Bull*
This exquisite photograph of Norma Shearer shows her in the guise of Elizabeth Barrett in The Barretts of Wimpole Street in which she appears with Fredric March and Charles Laughton

When you see this scene on the screen, remember that you too it being model. The camera is in the upper left hand corner with Director Sidney Franklin sitting beside it, the fellow adjusting the lights, while on the debris seat of the carriage is which Norma is riding on attache-with a huge elevator sunshade which he has held. Directly in front of him is the microphone, shaped like a Lorelie and catching the sound at the booms

The BARRETTS of WIMPOLE STREET

Drop me a line

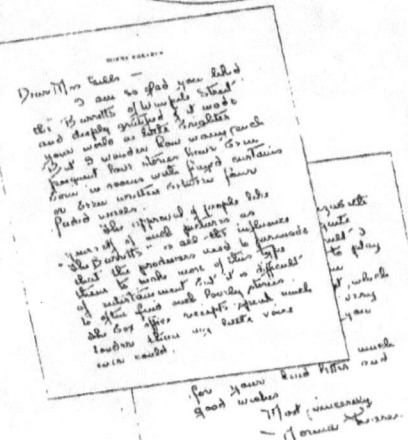

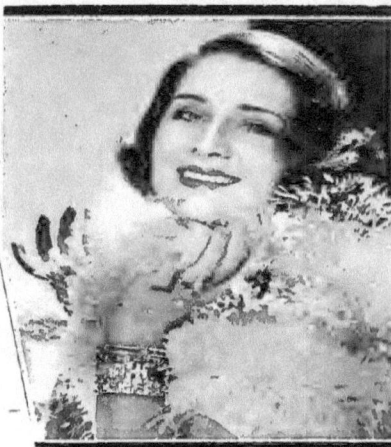

Norma Shearer

Norma Shearer's Answer

DEAR MRS GILLS:
I am so glad you liked *The Barretts of Wimpole Street* and deeply gratified if it made your world a little brighter. But I wonder how many such poignant love stories have been born in rooms with frayed curtains or even written between four faded walls.

The approval of people like yourself of such pictures as *The Barretts* is all the influence that the producers need to persuade them to make more of this type of entertainment but it is difficult to often find such lovely stories. The box office receipts speak much louder than my little voice ever could.

I loved the rôle of *Elizabeth Barrett*, although it was quite one of the most difficult I have ever been given to play. I think I will be in *Marie Antoinette* next, which is another rôle to be very grateful for. I hope you will like it.

Thank you so much for your kind letter and good wishes.

Most sincerely,
NORMA SHEARER.

Thanks to Norma Shearer
$10.00 Letter

MY DEAR NORMA SHEARER:
I have just seen *The Barretts of Wimpole Street* and am still under the spell. The faded wall paper and frayed curtains of the dingy rooms I call home actually seem to have an air of perked up freshness. Everything seems gayer, all because of this fine old love story. Please use your influence to have produced other charming stories of such lovely ethereal beauty. The world may change but it will always love romance and lovers.

After seeing you in *the Barretts of Wimpole Street*, I know this is the kind of rôle you love. What enjoyment you must have gotten from making the picture—am I not right? Have you any idea what type your next picture will be? Here's hoping it is something nice like the others. Lots of luck and happiness.

Your devoted fan,
MRS. B. R. GILLS,
235 Hood Street, Lynchburg, Va.

HOLLYWOOD SCRAPBOOK

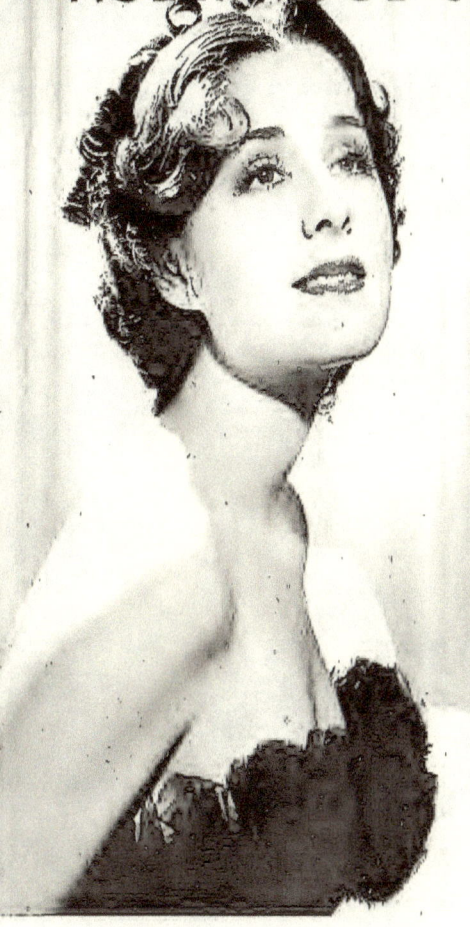

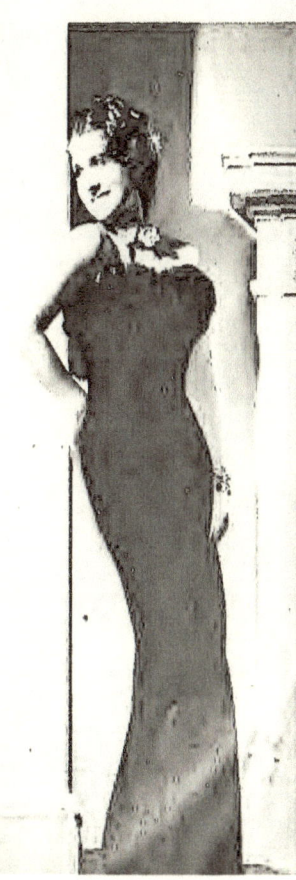

Norma Shearer

is at the present taking a vacation from the screen preparatory to another blessed event in the family. Meantime, Husband Irving Thalberg is considering a new release of "Smilin' Through" to appease the demands of Shearer fans for a current film. The shy poetess of "The Barretts of Wimpole Street" will later appear as the famous French queen in "Marie Antoinette," under the direction of Sidney Franklin.

● The coming big event in the Thalberg household will be the second. Norma retired once before to prepare for the arrival of Irving, Jr., and later returned to the screen to score new successes.

● Norma Shearer, Hollywood's symbol for success, has won the admiration of her own friends and acquaintances for her perfect serenity of soul. She possesses no desperate philoso-phies. She is content with whatever life brings her.

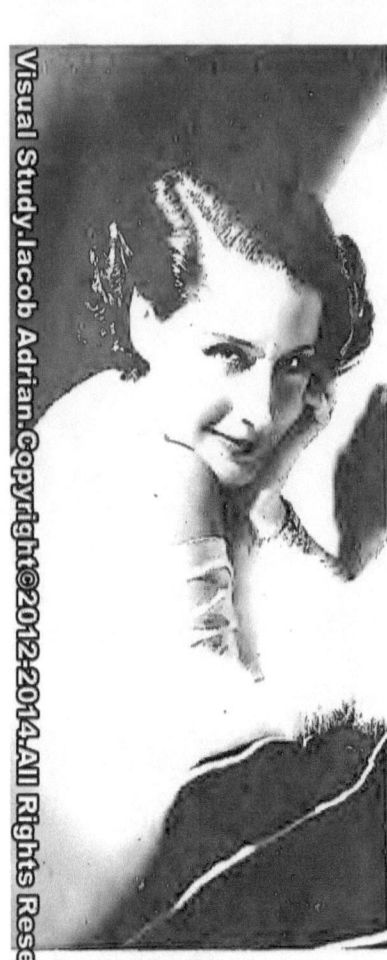

WHY I AM A NORMA SHEARER FAN *by Sally Eilers*

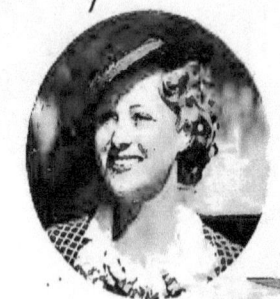

Norma Shearer's magnetic personality holds sway not only over millions of theatre goers, but Hollywood notables themselves. Sally Eilers tells you why

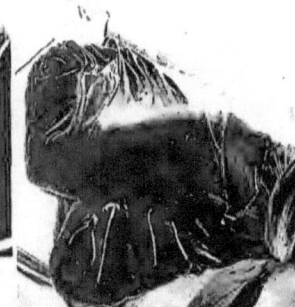

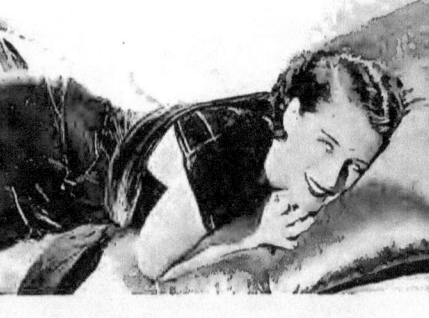

Only recently the mother of a second child—this time a daughter—Norma Shearer is again making plans for her return to the screen. In circle, Sally Eilers

THERE ARE very few people in the world who live completely within themselves. Most of us have ideals—someone we create with the perfections we hope to compensate in some small degree for our own imperfections. We live, I believe, not so much in what we are, as what we desire to be.

Norma Shearer is my ideal actress. Ever since I first saw her in *He Who Gets Slapped* with the late Lon Chaney, she has been my favorite. I met her for the first time during my extra days—when I was called to the set of one of her early films, and from that time on my admiration became something more than a "fan crush"— until today it is an almost idolic worship for a person who embodies all of the perfection I have ever hoped for.

This confession will, I am sure, come as a complete surprise to Norma Shearer herself, if she should happen to read it. It is because I stand in such real awe of her, I could never have her as a personal friend. The horizon recedes as we advance toward it. An ideal is like that—you can never come too close to it.

You remember Norma Shearer's *Let Us Be Gay*. Perhaps, you will remember I played one of the principals in that cast. That was my first opportunity to meet her personally. She was kind and gracious to me. She still is—today—when we meet at the homes of mutual friends. She never neglects coming over to speak to me—and I— well, I'm like any fan who suddenly comes face to face with their favorite film star—I just can't talk.

A typical instance of that occurred at a Mayfair party. It will seem amusing to you, but I assure you I was most embarrassed. She approached me in her usual, congenial manner, greeted me graciously and commented on how nice I looked. I blushed profusely, spluttered about for words, and finally stammered:

"—er—you're welcome!"

Imagine my confusion if you can.

● HAD IT been someone else other than Norma Shearer, I'm certain I could have managed something more eloquent—but, well—it was Norma Shearer.

Certainly as an actress she has been given no more applause or commendation than she deserves. Every inch of the way she has proven herself. She has never waited for breaks to come to her. She has worked with a tireless energy toward the goal she herself has set—and she has attained it through that self alone.

It is a pleasure to work with her on the set. She never tries to take advantage of her position as

Stars Own Stories

THE MOTION PICTURE THAT IS
EAGERLY AWAITED THE WORLD OVER

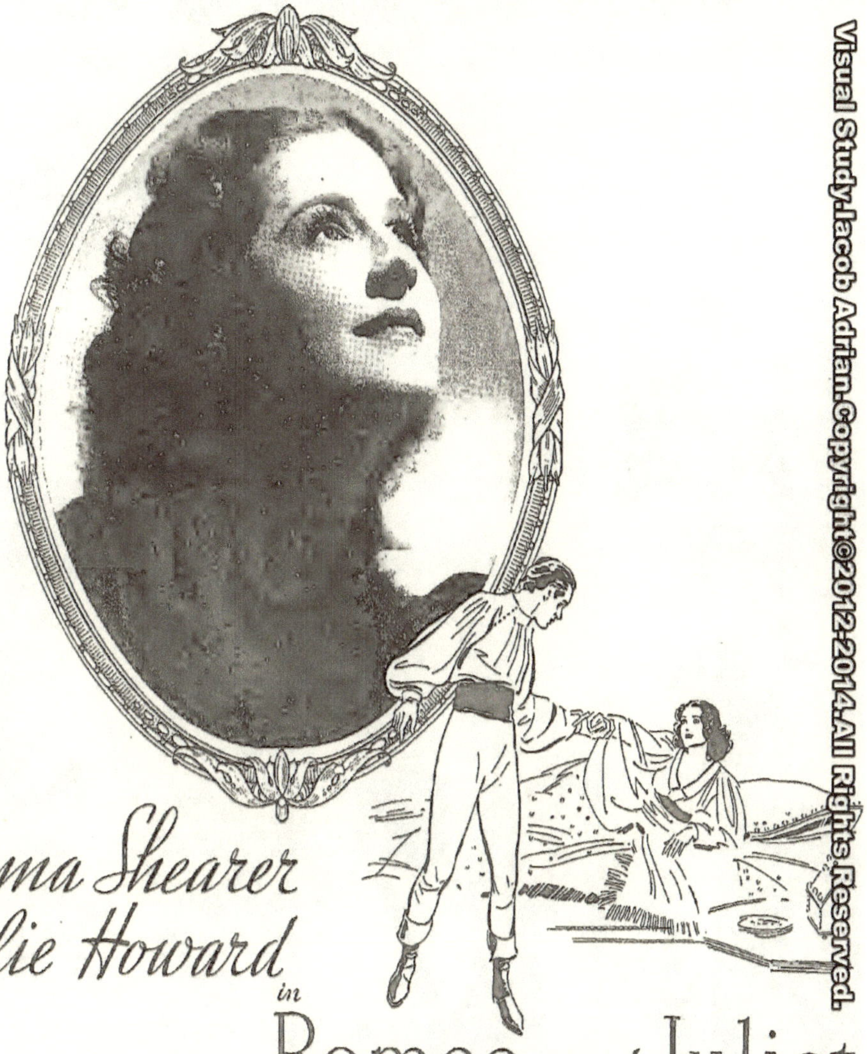

Norma Shearer
Leslie Howard

in

Romeo *and* Juliet

with

JOHN BARRYMORE

EDNA MAY OLIVER · VIOLET KEMBLE-COOPER
BASIL RATHBONE · CONWAY TEARLE
REGINALD DENNY · RALPH FORBES
C. AUBREY SMITH · HENRY KOLKER · ANDY DEVINE

To the famed producer Irving Thalberg go the honors for bringing to the screen, with tenderness and reverence, William Shakespeare's imperishable love story. The director is George Cukor. A METRO-GOLDWYN-MAYER PICTURE.

Juliets I HAVE KNOWN

by

Basil Rathbone

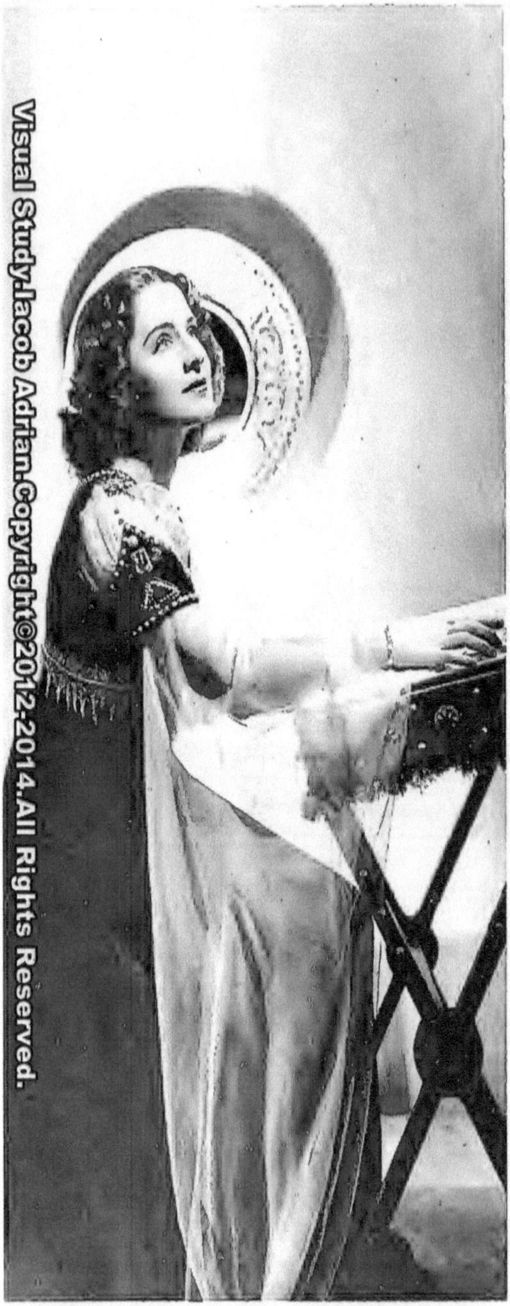

It Is August 1913 in Stratford-on-Avon. I stand at the stage door of the old Memorial Theatre. Looking down into the river I see myself dressed in a black costume of the 15th Century and holding in my arms a large bouquet of big white calla lilies. In a few minutes I shall lay my flowers at Juliet's tomb, cross swords with Romeo and, in the rule of Paris, pass into the records of my beloved profession, humbly taking my place in the history of the Stratford Festivals.

From upstream the river comes to me like a song I must have heard in some other life of a deep longing. Slowly and sweetly it is passing under the bridge bearing on its cool breast two proud white swans. They glide by me, and on down stream past Stratford Church, the burial place of William Shakespeare whom, God rest, has given me this most exquisite moment of realization.

My "call" comes and I go into the theatre and up onto the stage. On a bier, lighted by four tall candles lies Juliet, my first Juliet whom I love with all my heart and to whom I hardly ever speak, except in my part, for fear she shall break my dream. She never did. Even now I never think of her as Dorothy Green but as my first Juliet.

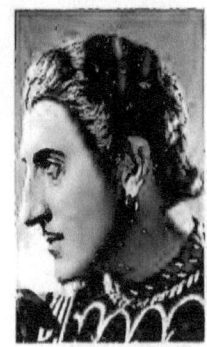

BASIL RATHBONE

● One Year Later! Malvern Wostershire. I am dressed in red and gold. I am standing in Juliet's garden looking up at her as she steps out onto her balcony to commune with me and with the night which is so completely ours, and ours alone, despite the presence of a large audience. Where are you today, my second Juliet? You had a soft and gentle loveliness that I like to remember.

There is a town somewhere in the northern part of England. I can see it clearly in my mind's eye but, for the life of me, I cannot recall its name. However, "what's in a name: a rose by any other name would smell as sweet." So let it be. It is time to go to the theatre. A deep glow from the setting sun gives this smoky city an illusive loveliness that I am sure reality denies it! I wanted to play Romeo so very [Continued on page 61]

Norma Shearer . . . . he had dreamed of such a Juliet

Romeo and Juliet are old friends of Basil Rathbone . . . . he having played Romeo more than 500 times on the stage . . . , wide-shouldered and narrow-hipped, Rathbone looks trim in tights . . . in the screen version he plays the rôle of Tibalt, cousin of Juliet, a fiery hot-headed young duelist who is ultimately killed by Romeo (Leslie Howard) . . . . to become thoroughly proficient, he dueled daily for 80 days before production began, and is as handy with the rapier as he is with the pen . . . this story was written by Rathbone expressly for HOLLYWOOD

Reviews of the Previews
by Top Hat . . . his expression tells the story

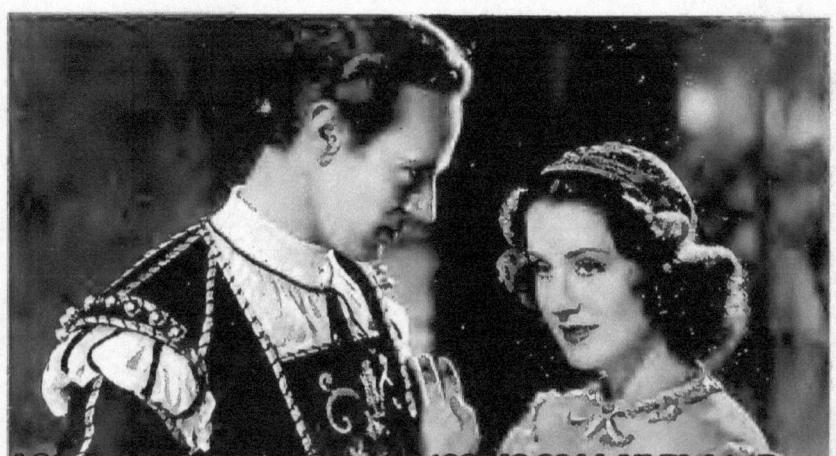

Norma Shearer and Leslie Howard are two of the stars in M-G-M's tremendous film, *Romeo and Juliet* which was previewed at one of Hollywood's biggest theaters with the public barred

ROMEO AND JULIET—(M-G-M)—A special showing of the $2,000,000 *Romeo and Juliet* to the press convinced those who have watched this film in the making that it tops all previous efforts of the industry in acting, photography, sets, costumes, music and all the allied talents of the picture business. For Norma Shearer it cannot help but bring the academy award, and all the huzzahs and honors an appreciative public may devise. Shakespeare gave Juliet all the best lines. Miss Shearer has read them beautifully. Romeo still dies beside her in the tomb, and Juliet still sheathes his dagger in her lovely breast, and the tragedy of these lovers still bring tears as it did when first presented in London in 1596. Incredible care went into the production. The balcony scene alone required five weeks to film, a month went into the making of the dueling scenes. While no ordinary mortal could have been considered perfect for everyone's notion of a Romeo, Leslie Howard does well by the rôle. Basil Rathbone, himself a noted Romeo of the stage, is as brilliant as a black diamond in the part of Tybalt, John Barrymore is a mad scapegrace of a Mercutio, while Edna Mae Oliver and all the others made of this play a grand and noble thing of beauty.

GIVE ME YOUR HEART—(Warners)— Built of stirring, human stuff, here is a film certain to tug at the hearts of all adults— it not being intended for child consumption. The problem: the unwed girl (Kay Francis) is about to become a mother. Her lover (Patric Knowles) is an English nobleman, married to an invalid wife (Frieda Enescort). Should Kay keep the child herself, or give it to her lover to raise as his own legitimate son? Her decision, and its consequences, make this a dramatic picture dealing largely with the neurosis which threatens the mother's happiness. George Brent and Roland Young are the other principal members of the cast, with Young doing one of his finest rôles to date. You will find Miss Francis handling her difficult assignment in marvelous style throughout most of the film. The drama of her problem, and the humor of Young's efforts to help her, are the highlights of the picture. Keep your eyes on Frieda Enescort.

WHITE FANG—(20th Century-Fox)—Additional melodrama of the Alaskan frontier, based along the lines of *Call of the Wild*, make this picture all right for summer entertainment. Michael Whalen, as the wrongly suspected young hero, is about to be hanged for killing his sweetheart's brother. Combined loyalties of his beloved (Jean Muir), and his comrade (Slim Summerville), save him from such a fate. John Carradine, as the menace, is worth a barrel of old fashioned hisses. In fact, they made him just a little too melodramatic. Charles Winninger (Remember him in *Showboat?*) is excellent as the old doctor.

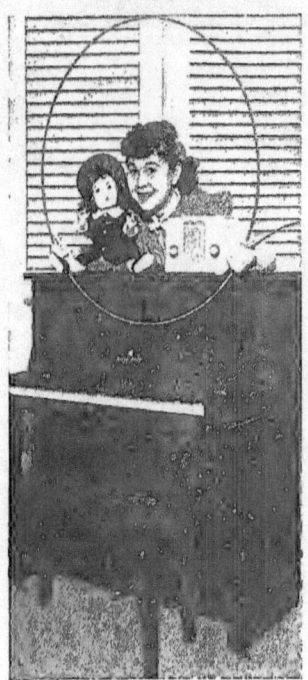

Jane Withers smiles over the top of the miniature piano which she will present to the clever winner of her "Miss Santa Claus" contest. Second prize is the pretty little radio, and third is the Jane Withers doll. The hoop, Jane is keeping for herself. Because of the great number of answers, winners will not be announced until next month's issue

For OUR GANG simply dotes on it . . . now.

THE GANG, it seems, was summoned to the studio to make some Thanksgiving pictures for publicity purposes. "Aw," they grumped, "it's nuthin' but a lotta hooey . . . prop turkeys and no fun."

But a surprise awaited them. The pictures were to be made in color. And as color picks up as black-and-white does not, real food had to be used.

Presto, chango . . . roasted brown turkeys made their appearance, with cranberry sauce and pies and all the wotnots that accompany a turkey dinner! The kids have been clamoring for more publicity pictures ever since.

A letter from MAUREEN O'SULLIVAN, now in England playing the leading feminine role in A Yank At Oxford, discloses that she and husband JOHN FARROW are living in a small cottage in the town of Denham, only a few minutes' walk from the studio . . . and the house was built in 1561.

Further . . . the entire troupe uses elaborate trailers for dressing rooms. And, one day, while motoring through the country at a leisurely pace, she chanced to look behind and there were fifteen or sixteen people on bicycles following her. When they saw she noticed them, all—as of one accord—waved to her.

W. S. VAN DYKE, the director, delights in baiting people. NELSON EDDY is his latest victim.

A certain woman writer for an important syndicate wrote something about the two that neither particularly liked. They got together, and agreed that neither would henceforth have anything to do with this individual, and they'd make things as tough as possible for her.

Came the day she arrived on the set. "I won't work with that woman here," EDDY declared. He stalked away for a few moments, then returned.

There, chatting and laughing uproariously, sat VAN DYKE and the writer, the best of friends. EDDY, now, trusts NO ONE.

LITTLE LOOK-SEES: HAROLD LLOYD is taking unto himself new fame, as The Great Clayton. In the event this title means nothing to you . . . LLOYD has turned mind-reader—for social purposes, of course—but it's reported that his talent along this line is positively amazing.

CONSTANCE BENNETT has gone into the cosmetics business, and you'll probably be using her product yourself before long. Her brand is shortly to go on the market in every prominent city of the United States.

OLIVER HARDY, of LAUREL and HARDY, can't play Bridge unless there's a platter—yes, platter—of sandwiches by his side. Whenever he enters a game at the club, a waiter always hovers near to see that the platter is never empty.

FRANCES LANGFORD has started a "friendship garden" along the side of her new Brentwood home. It will be used exclusively for flowers and plants given her by her friends. Already, there are more than fifty different varieties of rare plants.

FRED ASTAIRE has copyrighted the Drum Dance he has devised for Damsel In Distress. More than twenty drums of rather mammoth proportions are used in this sequence, and 'tis reported it is one of the most novel dancing numbers ever viewed.

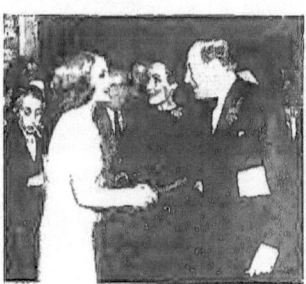

Norma Shearer, just beginning to appear in public again, greets Dolores Del Rio and Gregory Ratoff before a Philharmonic concert

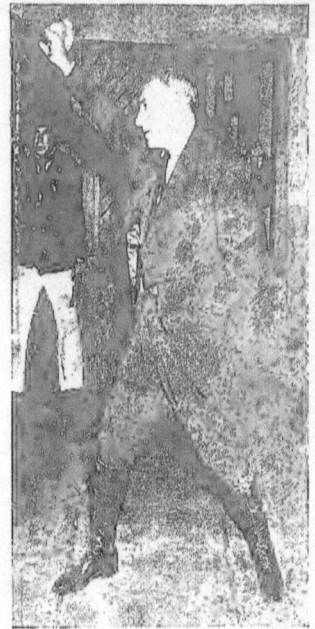

As usual, Cecil De Mille does as much acting as anyone in the cast of the film he is producing. Here he is in full action, testing the stool of a sword to be used by Fredric March in his role of the colorful pirate, La Fitte, in The Buccaneer. He borrowed the 19th century tail coat from his star to help him get in the proper swash-buckling mood

Because she failed to heed the warning of a studio make-up artist, LILY PONS found herself immersed in trouble.

For several of the scenes in her latest picture, Lily had to wear body make-up. A new type of make-up was used, one on which water had no effect. A special remover was required to divest the wearer of this make-up. Moreover, water turned the make-up into a hard cake, and almost impossible to remove.

Well, sir, Lily forgot all about this, and when the day's work was done dashed to her dressing room and under the shower. And therein lies our tale.

Three women labored over Lily for more than an hour, in an effort to remove the cakey substance that covered almost her entire body. Lily, at last reports, had put herself completely in the hands of her make-up artist.

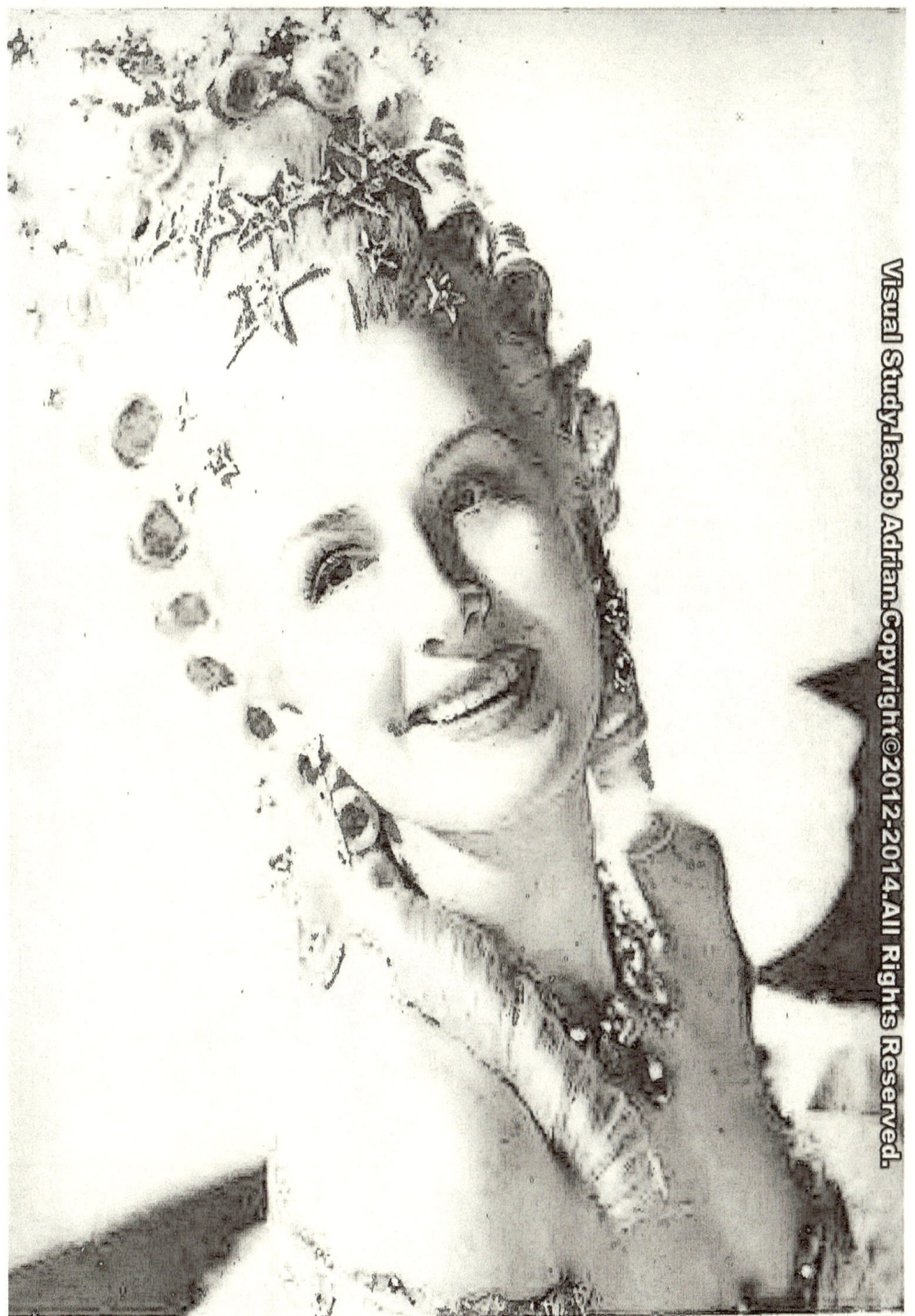

NORMA SHEARER

Radiantly lovely is the star in the powdered wig, the lavish laces and the splendid jewels of *Marie Antoinette* who lived so gaily and who died with such tragic gallantry. The film will be one of the most important of early fall releases from the Metro-Goldwyn-Mayer Studios

Laugh It Off

hardest, is when she's built herself up to having a pretty good opinion of herself.

"I'll never forget the time," she says, "when I got a pretty good opinion of myself as a tennis player. For months I took lessons from a professional coach, Eleanor Tennant. Sure that I was another Alice Marble, I challenged my husband, Jack Pressman, to a set. He beat me soundly, and I found that my ego was slightly bent.

■ There have been other laughs, too—that time she drove through a stoplight very slowly because there were no cars coming in either direction. The inevitable cop bounced out of the inevitable hideaway, eyed her, and said:

"Say—you're Claudette Colbert, aren't you?"

She nodded very sweetly, and said that she was. She was thinking that getting out of this ticket was a pushover, and she began courting the idea that it was nice to be known.

The policeman had seen several of her pictures and commented on them. In fact, he and she had a grand time for about ten minutes. After a while, he said:

"Now, if you'll just give me your license, I'll fill out your ticket."

And he did. The blow to Claudette's vanity was quite a something. But she laughed and the cop laughed, and she drove away.

"The ticket was a lesson in not feeling too important, and the laugh was the tonic that took the sting off the lesson," she says.

Claudette is mighty grateful to such pictures as *The Gilded Lily, The Bride Comes Home, I Met Him In Paris, Tovarich,* and now, *Bluebeard's Eighth Wife.*

"You have to be able to laugh at yourself before others will laugh at you. To make people laugh, you have to surrender to the idea of making yourself appear ridiculous. And anyone who makes himself appear ridiculous deliberately hasn't much chance to develop a superiority complex.

"This is true in pictures. And it's always true in real life, too. No blow is so great, whether it is mental or physical, that it can't be laughed into good fortune —if you laugh hard enough, and if you mean it."

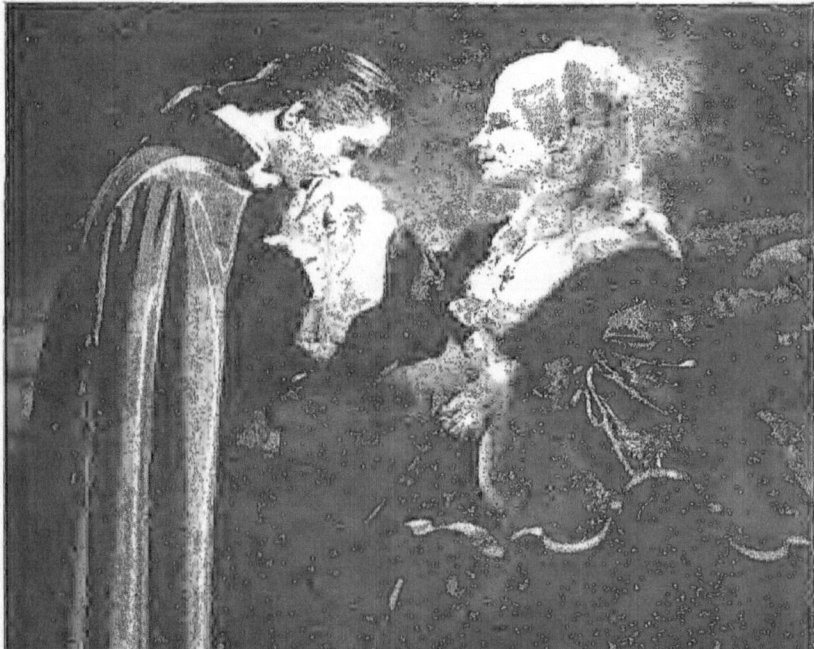

One of the highly dramatic scenes in *Marie Antoinette* is when the stately queen, played by Norma Shearer, greets the romantic young Count Fersen, acted by Tyrone Power. The production, one of the biggest to come from M-G-M this year, will be ready for release in the early fall

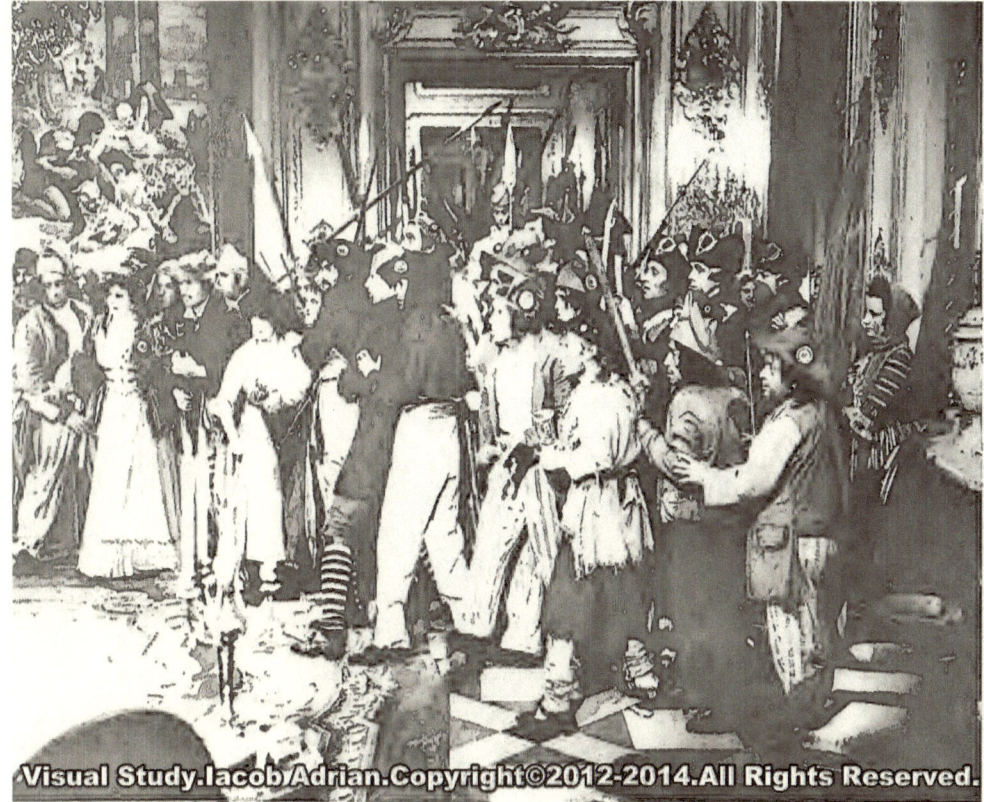

The exquisite Marie Antoinette knew only vaguely that there was starvation in France, and misery and injustice, until a rabble, such as the one pictured above, burst into her palace. Norma Shearer plays the colorful life of the tragic queen

A Day With a Queen

Here is an absorbing report of one day spent on the set during filming of *Marie Antoinette*

By JESSIE HENDERSON

Marie Antoinette was fed up, trying to get married. Finally she laughed, plumped down on the scarlet cushion that lay on the altar steps, heaped her hoop skirts in a diamond-sparkle froth, and hugged her knees. The Dauphin (Louis-Sixteenth-to-be) slid out of his splendid ermine cape and lighted a cigarette.

"Save the candles!" shouted Director William S. Van Dyck.

A grip in overalls flitted through the Versailles palace chapel and, using a hooded contraption on a long rod, began to kill the gigantic candles behind the carved stone altar. Plop! went each orange flicker of light, and shadows deepened around the wedding party. Marie Antoinette leaned her chin on a hand that flamed with jewels. This was the fourth attempt she and Louis had made to get married that afternoon. Something went haywire on each occasion.

"These royal weddings take time," observed Marie Antoinette-Norma Shearer with a smile.

"Back in the 1770's they negotiated three years for it," admitted the Dauphin bridegroom resignedly. He's Robert Morley, the personable young actor whom M-G-M "discovered" not long ago in England.

Just now the delay in the nuptials was due to a camera angle. So the entire French court relaxed right where it stood, flopping to the floor in a rustle of taffeta and a clink of swords. The Dauphin strolled outside for a bottle of lemon pop. The bride, pausing for a word with brother Douglas Shearer, chief sound technician for M-G-M, went billowing away to her portable dressing-room that was equipped with garage doors eight feet wide to accommodate those farflung hoops. She had every right to rest between takes. Norma weighs 110 pounds, and the silver and jewel studded wedding gown, plus train, weighed 108!

While, for a very special shot, the camera crew tinkered over gadgets eighty feet above the sound stage, the French court broke into animated talk. They chattered casually of things that would have made the original French court's powdered hair stand on end in superstitious

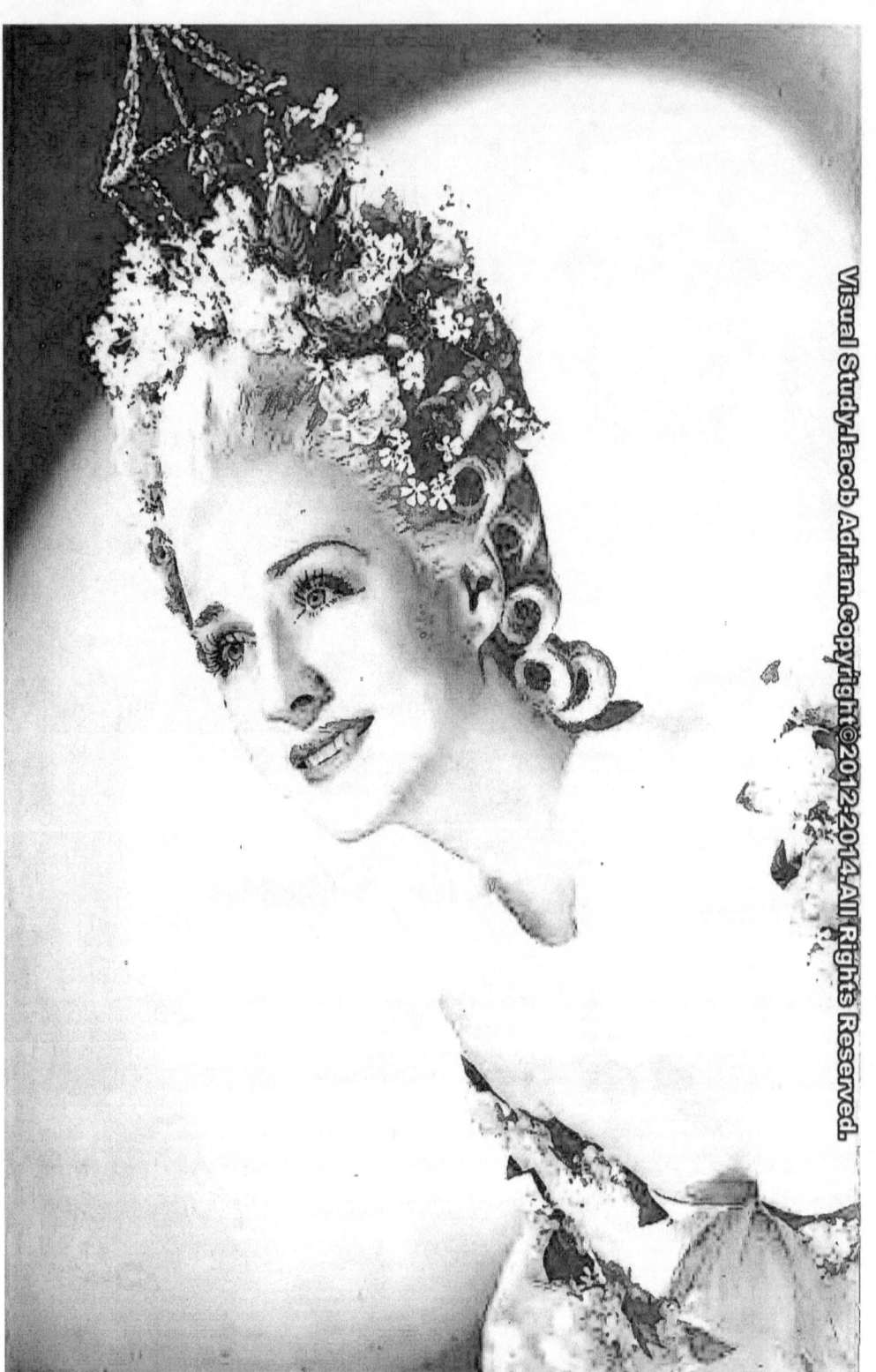

A Day With a Queen

awe—such things as telephone calls, the radio, last night's movie.

Following the Dauphin out to the soft drink stand, went a figure in sober gray and black. That man could have given Louis at least a hint as to the electric age to come. Benjamin Franklin, intent at the moment on a beaker of buttermilk while awaiting his own appearance in a later scene, was—you recall—the man who sent up a kite in a Philadelphia thunderstorm in order to learn about electricity. He didn't introduce radio to the French court during his visit there as envoy from the infant United States, but he's the grand-dad of radio just the same. And of all modern electrical items, including the movies.

As in Quaker hues he rubbed elbows with the rich plush and satin of French nobility, somebody exclaimed how Walter Walker (that is "Benjamin Franklin") had made himself up to look exactly like the picture of Franklin on a hundred-dollar bill. I wouldn't know about this. But I do know that Robert Morley in make-up so resembles the true Louis Sixteenth that they don't mind photographing him side by side with an authentic portrait of the monarch.

■ Behind Louis Sixteenth and Franklin, and headed toward the ice cream wagon, came Louis the Fifteenth, grandfather and predecessor of Louis the Sixteenth and sponsor of the latter's marriage. Despite the heliotrope brocade, he was unmistakably John Barrymore. When Norma first saw him on the set she forgot her lines; not account of the heliotrope brocade but account of admiration. She'd never met him before! No fooling.

Since her own start in pictures he had been one of her great favorites of stage and film. Once, in the earlier days, they were working in adjoining sets and Norma, then nearly unknown, used to dart out the back way and over to his set in order to watch him from afar. But they had never happened to meet. Not even during the production of *Romeo and Juliet*, for they didn't appear in the same scenes.

Louis Fifteenth was joined at the ice cream wagon by the Duc d'Orleans (Joseph Schildkraut), the meanie of Marie's reign, all the time stirring up trouble. And by Mme. la Motte, as played by Mae Busch of the silent cinema. Norma, because she also hero-worshipped this actress when Mae was a star and Norma only a beginner, sent her own car to bring Mae to the studio when tests of her for the role were to be made.

■ Lafayette sauntered up for a strawberry ice cream cone, followed by a detachment of the Swiss guard on the same errand. Here came the studio trolley that ambles about the lot and debouched a lady in waiting, her emerald skirts carefully spread. Hopping briskly to the ground she lifted the hoops high to avoid the dust. Everybody roared. It was a rather cool day and beneath the hoops she was wearing bright red slacks. They looked like flannel underwear.

The sight mightily intrigued the royal choir boys grouped nearby. They whistled in unison, to the lady's confusion. These little tykes, short brown wigs forever wildly a-flying, pulled more tricks daily than a harried supervisor could anticipate, stopped the heartbeats of the wardrobe department by shinnying fire escapes in their white surplices, and intermittently at the proper signal turned their faces heavenward and broke into beatific song.

■ I was having a root beer with the Princesse de Lamballe, Marie Antoinette's dearest f r i e n d (Anita Louise), in turquoise with mountainous plumes to match—when the nobility began to dash back to the sound stage for another go at the wedding. Norma and Morley had been sent for, but their standins still knelt before the altar, looking as if their knees were pretty tired of it all. To "Skats" Wyrick, ex-football star at UCLA, and stand-in for the Dauphin, somebody sympathetically handed a cigar and "Skats" was carefully keeping the ashes away from his blue velvet coat.

The Cardinal, in crimson robe, delicate lace and little round cap, sat fast asleep on a stool. Tyrone Power, the romantic "Count Fersen" of the picture, the young Swedish aristocrat whom Marie Antoinette loved, came suddenly through a doorway talking to Norma Shearer. Tyrone who had no part in this marriage scene, wore modern brown tweeds and probably couldn't realize how odd he looked next to a lady in a gown like a white balloon and a coiffure like piled-up soapsuds.

■ "Ready, baby?" inquired Director Van Dyck. He was speaking to Norma Shearer; and the first time he called her "baby" and "kid" everybody looked as horrified as if he were addressing Marie Antoinette herself. Everybody, that is, but Norma. She didn't mind at all.

Indeed, to this first picture she has made since the death of her husband, Irving Thalberg, (it is also the first picture in which Van Dyck has directed her), Norma brought her own brand of courage; the kind of courage that can smile. She left her private grief outside the sound stage door and, the moment she crossed the threshold—despite the sharp memories that must have tormented her —she became Norma Shearer the actress and the gracious friend. Almost the last time I had seen her was during a sequence of *Romeo and Juliet* when Irving Thalberg looked on so proudly as she danced in the great banquet hall of the Capulets.

"Ready!" she smiled now at Van Dyck and took her place before the chapel altar.

In accents like cream and Chinese gongs Nigel de Brulier as the Cardinal read the rolling Latin of the marriage service. "Okay," called Van Dyck, "But it is Greek to me! Can we have it in English?"

Nobody knew it in English. Scurry, scurry. Find a translator. Find a typewriter. Tap out the Latin lines in English and hand 'em quick to the Cardinal. Boy, will that pair NEVER get married?

Two wardrobe assistants brought a low stool for Marie Antoinette (the French court had once again dropped en masse to the floor) and arranged her wedding gown with its garlands of shirred ribbon so it wouldn't crumple.

■ Marie was fond of ornate clothes.

In this picture, the action of which covers twenty years, Norma wears 34 costumes, each over 52 pounds in weight, not to mention 18 wigs.

Each dress was draped over a steel hoop which in turn was fastened to a foundation so adjusted that the weight hung from the shoulders. The hoop had a petticoat under it, a second frilled petticoat fastened to it, and a much more frilled petticoat over it . . . although the ladies of the real French court are said to have worn no lingerie whatever, tsk, tsk. Moreover, Norma's wigs, and those of the others, had metal framework of considerable weight to keep them in shape. When the real Marie Antoinette held formal court, she wore a coiffure so lofty that a page had to follow behind with a wooden prop to hold it in place till she was settled in her chair of state.

"Which o n l y proves," commented Norma, "that a woman can get used to any kind of clothes!"

Incidentally, it took a lady of the French court, in this most extravagant epoch woman's dress has ever seen, a good five hours to climb into her formal apparel, including the coiffure. Thanks to talon fasteners for clothes and whatnots to hold wigs in place, an M-G-M lady of the French court could leap into her formal attire in five minutes.

■ Van Dyck summoned the principals once more to their wedding. The high, sweet chant of those impish choir boys arose. The English translation had come. Having been wed in Latin, Marie and Louis were now wed in English. And then, for good measure, in Latin again. . . .

Thoroughly married, they proceeded in the cockeyed but (believe it or not) efficient Hollywood manner to do the scene before the one just completed. That is to say, they next did the wedding procession which comes before the marriage. Two wardrobe women carried Norma's train as she disappeared beyond the entrance archway of the chapel. Organ music burst forth in a joyous strain. Slowly through the archway paced the bridal party, a tossing crest of pastel plumes, a following surf of brocade and velvet topped by a foam of white wigs with here and there a flash of jewelled sword hilt or of coronet.

The bride . . . if Norma thought at that moment of her own wedding day, or of how she and her husband together had planned this very picture for her there was no sign on that calm, faintly smiling face. She moved forward, the veil frosted with silver falling about her like a spent wave. And thus, cinematically, the 15-year-old Austrian Archduchess and the 16-year-old Dauphin who liked his blacksmith shop better than his palace, began what proved to be their march toward the guillotine. But that was twenty years ahead of them.

In the meantime, several days before the wedding scene was shot, they had filmed the sequence in which the royal couple's first child was born! Norma startled her own doctor who for some time had been eager to watch a movie in process of production. "Come right over to the studio," Norma telephoned him hurriedly one noon, "I'm going to have a baby. About two o'clock, they think. I mean—" He came right over.

And shortly after the birth of her child, Marie Antoinette—thanks to what can be done on celluloid—was dancing the minuet. One of the most dramatic as well as most magnificent minuets ever screened.

For it, the ballroom at the palace of Versailles had been reproduced from dear knows how m a n y photographs and sketches. Big enough to hold French royalty and a large slice of French history, the real ballroom wasn't colossal enough for Hollywood and camera angles. Hence, the one built on the M-G-M sound stage is 250 feet long and, 125 feet wide, about twice the width of the original.

They reproduced the grand staircase exactly; the crystal chandeliers like pyramids of ice; the marble pillars, brownish pink, with their gold encrustations; the famous ceiling in panels of rose, green and gold, its nude figures symbolizing whatever they symbolize. Filled with a rhythmic pattern of dancers that swept through the deliberate figures of the minuet, the room presented a spectacle so glowing and varied that the real French court could hardly have excelled it.

That dance was given, at the insistence of Louis Fifteenth, to end a feud between Marie Antoinette and Louis Fifteenth's girl-friend—Madame du Barry. Marie Antoinette had at length consented to "recognize" the du Barry socially by speaking to her in public instead of sailing past with nose in air. The music would stop, Marie Antoinette would edge over toward du Barry, and—say something. "What weather, Madame!" is the remark which history says Marie made.

The Duc d'Orleans was looking almost with apprehension at Marie Antoinette; the Duc—or, rather, Joseph Schildkraut—hadn't known how to dance till this picture when he took special lessons. First off, his rapier caught in Marie Antoinette's feathered gown while they practiced and the hoops flew up, the feathers w h i r l e d to her shoulders. "Clodhopper!" Van Dyck called him after

that, ribbing him unmercifully, telling people they had to follow him around the dance floor with needle and thread.

"Louis Sixteenth lived to be 39 years old, and he had 26 baths in his whole life," remarked George Richelavie pensively at my elbow. Richelavie, the technical advisor, knew everything about everything. "They were great events, those baths. He noted them in his diary."

In and out hurried a busy figure with dark, bobbed hair; the navy blue dress very utilitarian by contrast. Albertina Rasch, who from 600 applicants selected 64 couples and taught them the minuet in two days.

"Only 64 couples dance, but there are more than 500 people in this scene—" Richelavie began. He was interrupted by the measured beat of the minuet sounding for a rehearsal. Stately bows and curtsies; hands daintily uplifted, palm outward; the pretty and delicious artificialty of the gentry of the age. No Benny Goodman. No—my gosh!—big apple.

"All right!" Van Dyck called through the loud speaker, "now for the real thing. Camera! And you, Schildkraut, keep your big feet off Shearer's dress." He spoke to the Queen of France. "Ready, baby?"

"Ready," said Norma. With grace the company advanced, retreated, glittered . . . *C'est la vie, hein?* While it lasted.

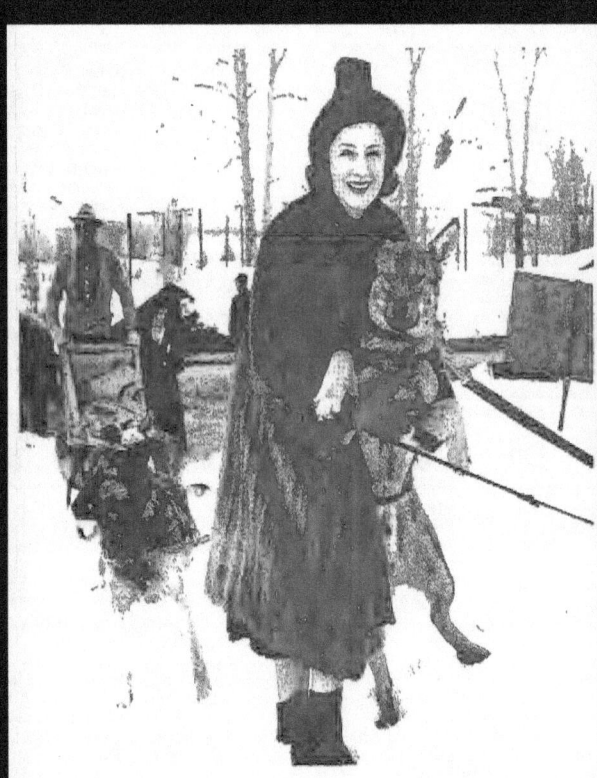

Norma Shearer likes a fast ride over the snow at Sun Valley behind a team of sled-dogs. Here she is with one of the Alaskan Huskies. Her next film is *Idiot's Delight,* soon to be released

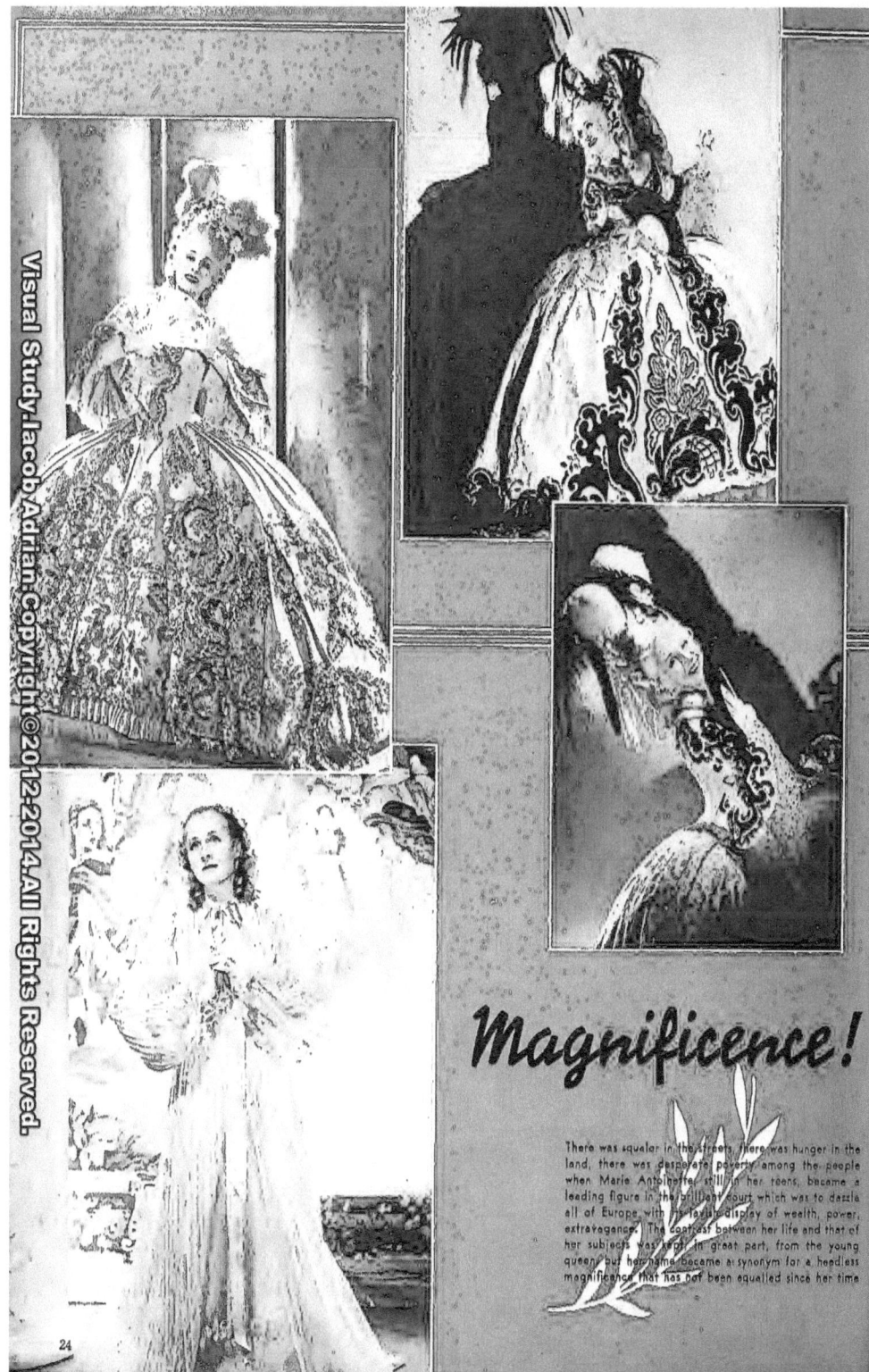

Magnificence!

There was squalor in the streets, there was hunger in the land, there was desperate poverty among the people when Marie Antoinette, still in her teens, became a leading figure in the brilliant court which was to dazzle all of Europe with its lavish display of wealth, power, extravagance. The contrast between her life and that of her subjects was kept, in great part, from the young queen, but her name became a synonym for a heedless magnificence that has not been equalled since her time

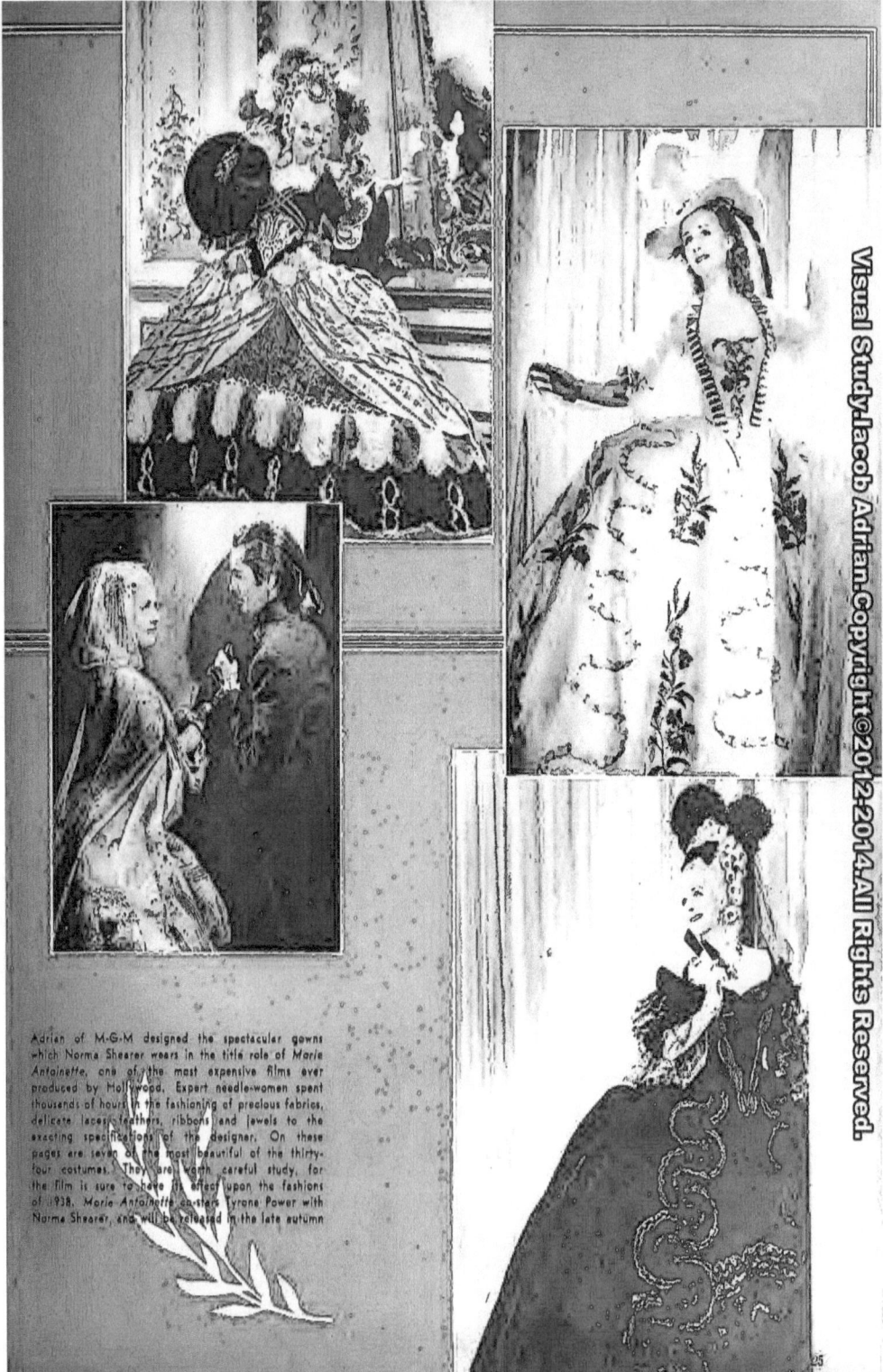

Adrian of M-G-M designed the spectacular gowns which Norma Shearer wears in the title role of *Marie Antoinette*, one of the most expensive films ever produced by Hollywood. Expert needle-women spent thousands of hours in the fashioning of precious fabrics, delicate laces, feathers, ribbons and jewels to the exacting specifications of the designer. On these pages are seven of the most beautiful of the thirty-four costumes. They are worth careful study, for the film is sure to have effect upon the fashions of 1938. *Marie Antoinette* co-stars Tyrone Power with Norma Shearer, and will be released in the late autumn

25

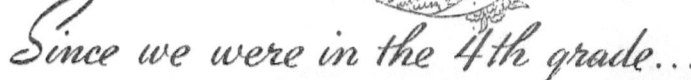

Since we were in the 4th grade...

All of us..kids together..we have been reading about Marie Antoinette..the glamorous Queen of France. Of her virtues..her intrigue and brilliance as a queen but ..more than anything else..we read of her scarlet history as the playgirl of Europe... of her flirtations..her escapades with the noblemen of her court..her extravagances even while her subjects starved. ✳ Now the screen gives us.."MARIE ANTOINETTE" the woman ..we see her, as tho' through a keyhole..not on the pages of history... but in her boudoir ..in the perfumed halls of the palace of Versailles. ..on the moonlit nights in her garden..A rendezvous with her lover ..we follow her through triumphs and glory..midst the pageantry of that shameless court..we see the tottering of her throne..the uprising of her people..her arrest and imprisonment..and we follow her on that last ride through the streets of Paris to the guillotine. NEVER..not since the screen found voice..has there been a drama so mighty in emotional conflict..so sublime in romance..so brilliant in spectacle..so magnificent in performance..truly "MARIE ANTOINETTE" reaches the zenith of extraordinary entertainment thrill!

NEVER HAS THE SCREEN
WITNESSED A GREATER
PERFORMANCE THAN
THAT OF NORMA SHEARER
AS THE "ROYAL BAD-GIRL"

NORMA   TYRONE
SHEARER · POWER
in Metro · Goldwyn · Mayer's Finest Motion Picture
The Private Life of
MARIE ANTOINETTE
JOHN BARRYMORE · ROBERT MORLEY
ANITA LOUISE · JOSEPH SCHILDKRAUT
Gladys GEORGE · Henry STEPHENSON
Directed by W. S. VAN DYKE II · Produced by HUNT STROMBERG

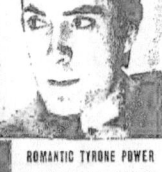

ROMANTIC TYRONE POWER
AS THE MAN WHO OFFERED
HER THE LOVE SHE
COULD NEVER FIND IN
HER STRANGE MARRIAGE

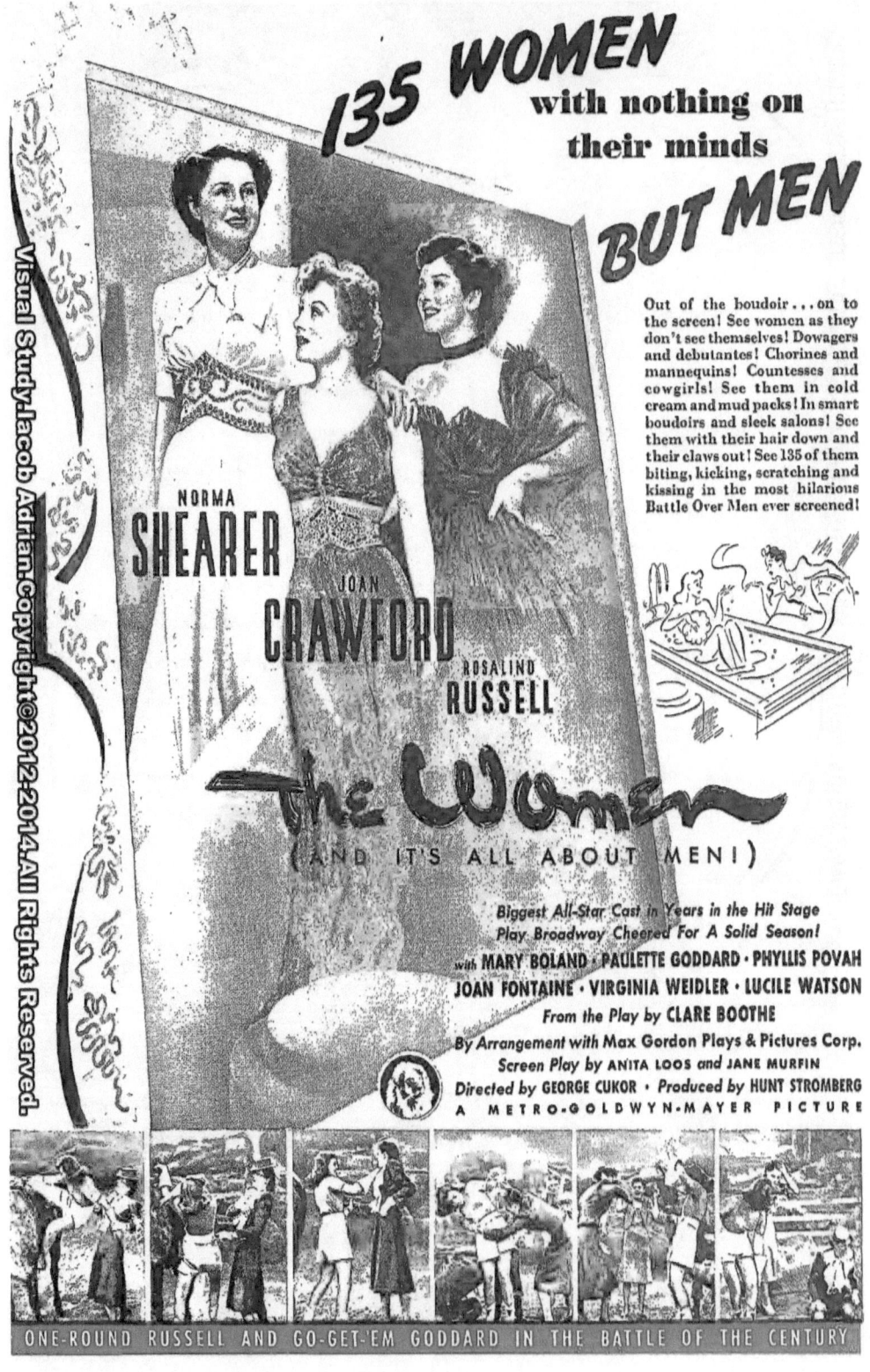

135 WOMEN
with nothing on their minds
BUT MEN

Out of the boudoir...on to the screen! See women as they don't see themselves! Dowagers and debutantes! Chorines and mannequins! Countesses and cowgirls! See them in cold cream and mud packs! In smart boudoirs and sleek salons! See them with their hair down and their claws out! See 135 of them biting, kicking, scratching and kissing in the most hilarious Battle Over Men ever screened!

NORMA
SHEARER

JOAN
CRAWFORD

ROSALIND
RUSSELL

The Women
(AND IT'S ALL ABOUT MEN!)

Biggest All-Star Cast in Years in the Hit Stage Play Broadway Cheered For A Solid Season!
with MARY BOLAND · PAULETTE GODDARD · PHYLLIS POVAH
JOAN FONTAINE · VIRGINIA WEIDLER · LUCILE WATSON
From the Play by CLARE BOOTHE
By Arrangement with Max Gordon Plays & Pictures Corp.
Screen Play by ANITA LOOS and JANE MURFIN
Directed by GEORGE CUKOR · Produced by HUNT STROMBERG
A METRO-GOLDWYN-MAYER PICTURE

ONE-ROUND RUSSELL AND GO-GET-'EM GODDARD IN THE BATTLE OF THE CENTURY

Escape

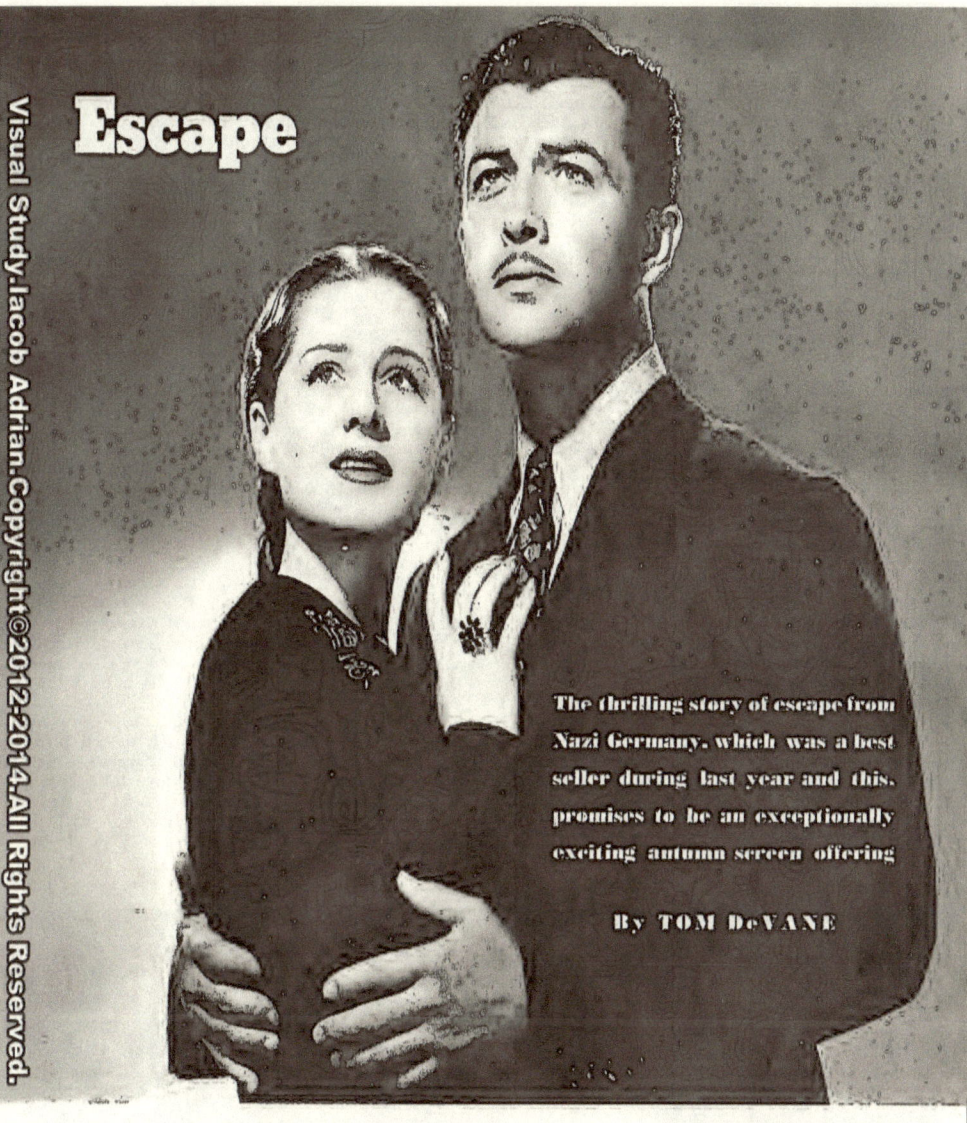

The thrilling story of escape from Nazi Germany, which was a best seller during last year and this, promises to be an exceptionally exciting autumn screen offering

By TOM DeVANE

The *Countess von Trenck* stepped out of her portable dressing room, the largest and flossiest these eyes have ever seen in a good many years of movie-set wandering. For one fleeting moment she held her regal pose—then she wriggled her nose, twinkled her eyes, and became Hollywood's own Norma Shearer.

It was between scenes on M-G-M's *Escape*, and obviously there was something in the air. Nearly all the set workers had stopped their labors, waiting for a signal from Miss Shearer, who was carrying an elaborately-wrapped package. She asked someone, "Where is he?" and was assured that "he" was in a corner of the set. "All right," beamed Norma, "let's start it!"

The sound man started the huge "playback" machine. Immediately the stage was filled with the enthusiastic strains of "Happy Birthday to You." Miss Shearer, bearing her package, took the arm of Mervyn LeRoy, producer-director of *Escape*. Others followed. Soon there was a long procession daisy-chaining its way to the corner of the stage, where an embarrassed Bill Cotton (Le Roy's assistant) was wishing that such things as birthdays had never been thought of.

Norma said simply, "Happy birthday from all the gang, Bill!" embraced him warmly and handed him the package. The

record (especially recorded by the whole troupe one day when Cotton was off the set) continued blaring forth its loving message, while everyone applauded.

That's Norma for you. In the midst of making one of the most important pictures of her career, in a role that would have most "serious" actresses who "live" their roles immersed in gloom (*Escape* is not the cheeriest story in the world) the star still finds time to have fun. What's more, she sets great store in birthdays.

Miss Shearer would have graced any party the day we visited M-G-M and *Escape*. To our masculine eyes, her heavy white wool cape, with gold scroll embroidery around [*Continued on page 48*]

Robert Taylor as the desperate man who tricks the Nazis into releasing his mother from prison camp. Norma Shearer as the courageous Countess who risks her life to help

Escape

its military collar—was stunning enough. But the lassie with us whispered excitedly, "See! It's a new trend! *Adrian is bringing back the cape!*" We were in the midst of an authentic style scoop, and didn't know it. The illustration on this page will give you an idea of what we mean. And how do you like Norma's new hair-do? She parts it in the center and wears it with two loose knots in the back. Bee-youtiful, we say.

Escape, as you probably know, is the famous Ethel Vance best seller in which M-G-M is presenting Miss Shearer with Robert Taylor as co-star and a distinguished cast headed by Nazimova, Conrad Veidt, Felix Bressart, Bonita Granville and Blanche Yurka. Mervyn LeRoy, that perennial boy-wonder of the cinema, is in charge of the works.

Although Miss Vance's novel naturally bears angry anti-Nazi sentiments, the studio is concentrating on the romantic and thrilling aspects of the plot. The romance between the Countess and young Mark Preysing (Robert Taylor) will be given more prominence in the screen version.

The main plot of *Escape*, however—the melodramatic and spine-tingling efforts of Emmy Ritter's son, Mark, and his friends to rescue the great actress from a concentration camp, remains just as thrilling as it was in the book.

Emmy Ritter, you see, was known as a great American actress, in spite of her German birth. Of recent years her home in New York had become a haven for refugees, all of whom she welcomed with open arms. She made the fatal mistake of returning to Germany to dispose of her property—eventually managing to smuggle the money out of the country. The Nazis no like—not for one minute. Emmy is thrown in the pokey and sentenced to hasty execution.

Before they have a chance to chop her head off, however, she gets appendicitis and has to have an operation. It is while she is lying between life and death, befriended only by the young doctor who performed the operation, that her son, Mark, arrives, searching for her. When his efforts to battle official Nazidom finally fail, he enlists the terrified aid of the American-born Countess, whom he had met romantically in New York.

In the role of Emmy Ritter, the great Alla Nazimova is making her "talkie" debut. The "talkie" should tip you off—Nazimova is known to movie fans of an earlier generation. She quit before the silver screen had a chance to talk back. Not that it mattered—the lady has starred with great success in Ibsen dramas all across the country for the past decade.

Nazimova giggles when she tells of her first day's work in pictures after all these years. "I knew what was going to happen," she told us, "but it was still a shock. They take me and put me in a coffin and nail the lid down!"

It was a very nice coffin, however—all done up for Nazimova—with extra heavy shoulder pads. And—of all things—a head rest, rather like the ones you see on barber chairs. Madame Nazimova didn't mind. "After all, Robert Taylor had to carry me to the coffin," she smiled. "Think how

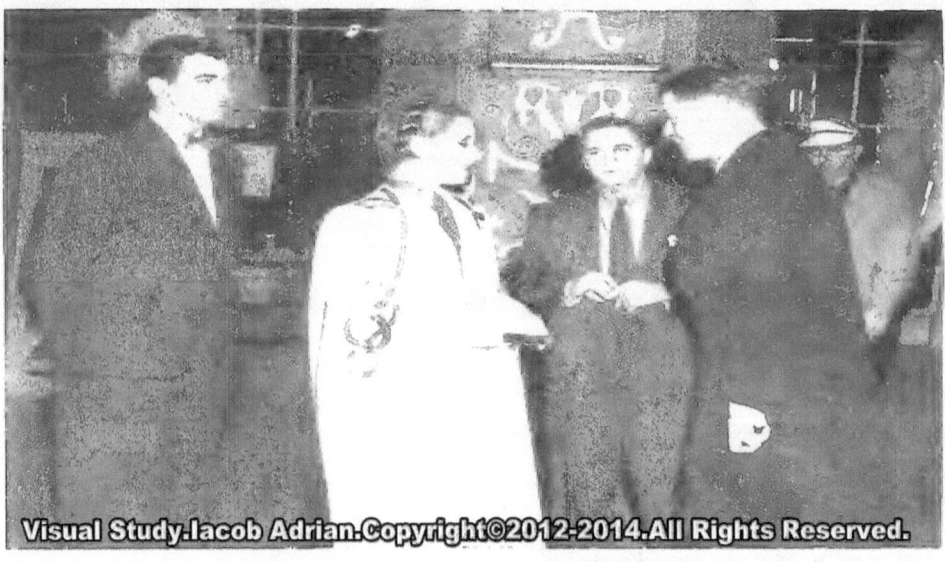

Norma Shearer, in the dramatic cape which is expected to set a new vogue, meets Philip Dorn who plays an important role in *Escape*. In the background, Robert Taylor and producer-director Mervyn LeRoy look with admiration at her hair-do

many women would want the same experience!"

The interviewer interrupted to tell Nazimova that the great Sarah Bernhardt used a coffin as a bed for many years. Mme. Nazimova's fragile body shook with laughter. "I went to sleep in mine, too, one night at the studio. But I do not like coffins for all the time."

The M-G-M grapevine insists that Nazimova will give a spectacular performance in *Escape*.

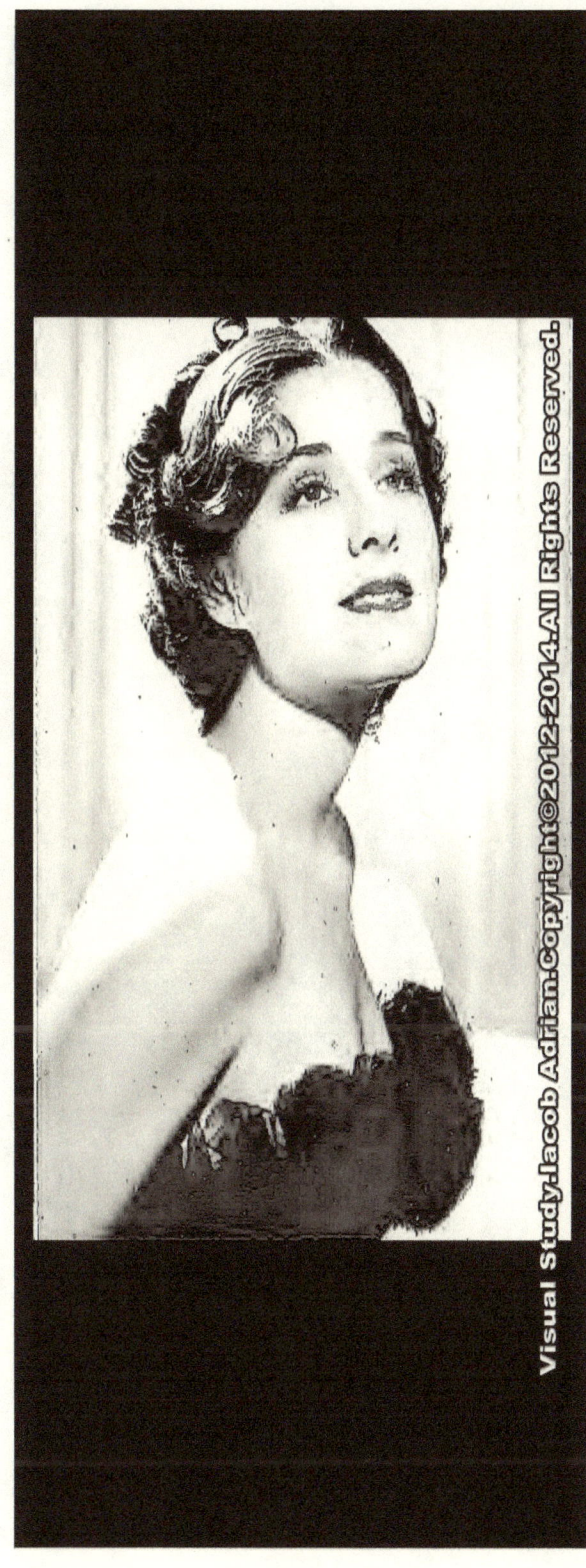

"I am a lucky woman," she says, seriously, "to return to the screen in such a good part. I've had other offers, of course. This studio wanted me to play *Madame de Farge* in *A Tale of Two Cities*. I was interested until they tell me that I am to have a knock-down fight with Miss Edna May Oliver. I mentally compare my size with that of Miss Oliver and I say, 'Oh! No!'" (Nazimova is slightly over five feet tall and a bit over one hundred pounds.)

"So I say to them, you should get a tall woman for that part. Why not try Blanche Yurka, that great woman, who would be wonderful? And they did, and she *was*.

"Yurka plays my prison nurse in *Escape*, you know. And she is so wonderful, that one. As long as I'm helpless in bed, I won't have to wrestle with her!"

Also in this same prison sequence is a young actor that the studio thinks will prove to be a hit. Just because we didn't know an Adrian style scoop when we face it, we'll tip you off to this one.

Philip Dorn is his name. In his native Holland, a few short years ago, he was known as the Clark Gable of the Netherlands. He played all of the typical Gable movie roles on the stage. You know—*Men in White* and *Idiot's Delight*. He was brought to this country some time ago by Joe Pasternak, the Universal producer who discovered Deanna Durbin and Gloria Jean. He was told to sit back in some cool dark spot and improve his English (it wasn't very bad when he arrived). So sit he did—and inside of six months his English was flawless. His screen debut was in *Ski Patrol*, and although the picture did not set box office fires, he made a personal hit.

Negotiations to borrow him from Universal proving unsuccessful M-G-M promptly pulled strings and bought his contract. And they have important plans for him. Dorn's no Arrow collar ad, but he has a lot of masculine oomph. Bet you'll like him.

In the role of the sinister *General* is the distinguished continental actor, Conrad Veidt. A star these many years (he was in the famous *Cabinet of Dr. Caligari*), Veidt is a stunning figure in his uniforms.

Robert Taylor still has the moustache so many girls think attractive. His *Escape* role should do a great deal to further his growing reputation as an actor of real ability. Personally, we're glad that his studio has given up its strenuous campaign to put him over as a junior edition of Wally Beery in the he-man roles. He's much more suited to sensitive, dramatic roles such as the one he had in *Waterloo Bridge* and in *Escape*.

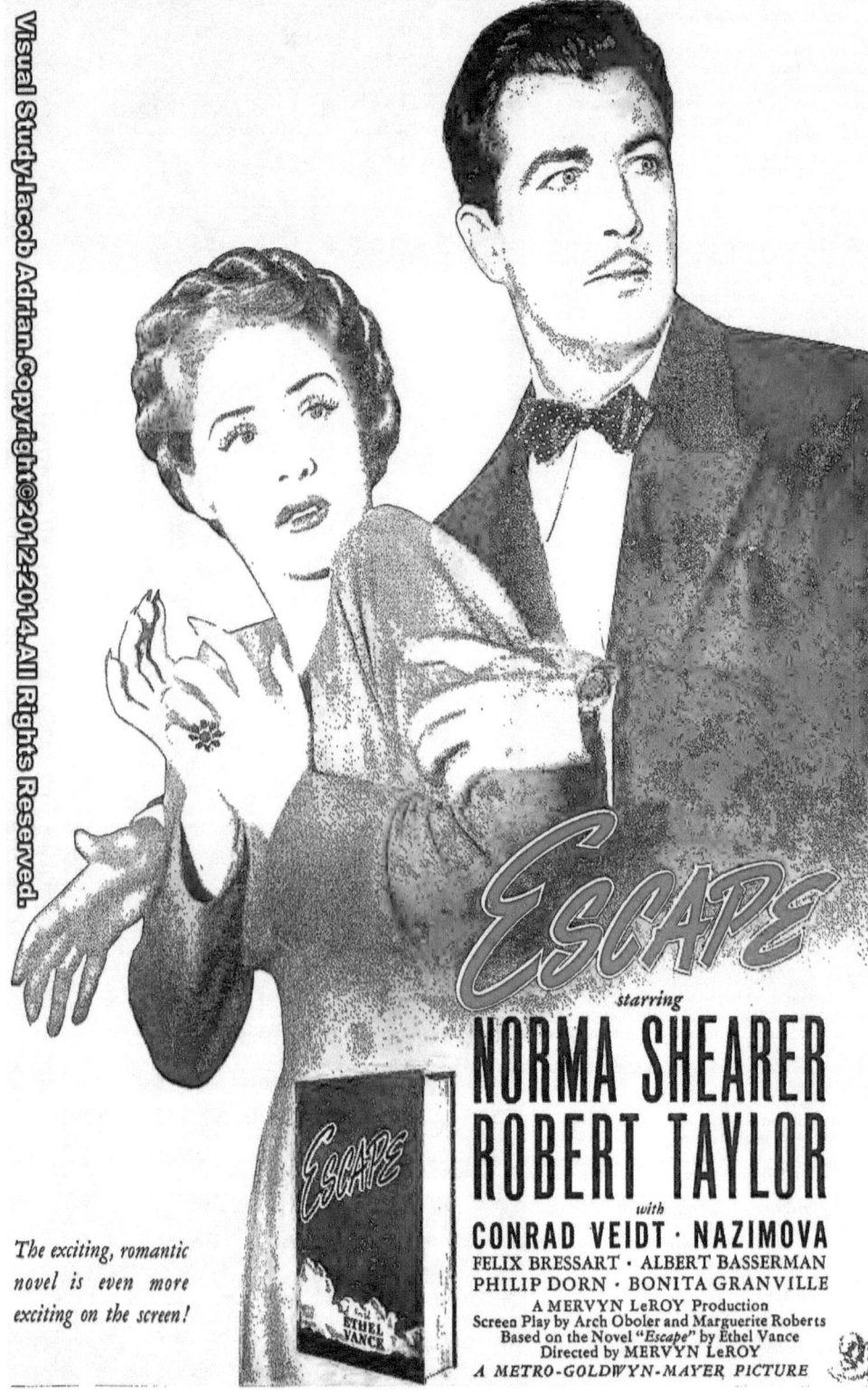

ESCAPE

starring

NORMA SHEARER
ROBERT TAYLOR

with

CONRAD VEIDT · NAZIMOVA

FELIX BRESSART · ALBERT BASSERMAN
PHILIP DORN · BONITA GRANVILLE

A MERVYN LeROY Production
Screen Play by Arch Oboler and Marguerite Roberts
Based on the Novel "*Escape*" by Ethel Vance
Directed by MERVYN LeROY

A METRO-GOLDWYN-MAYER PICTURE

The exciting, romantic novel is even more exciting on the screen!

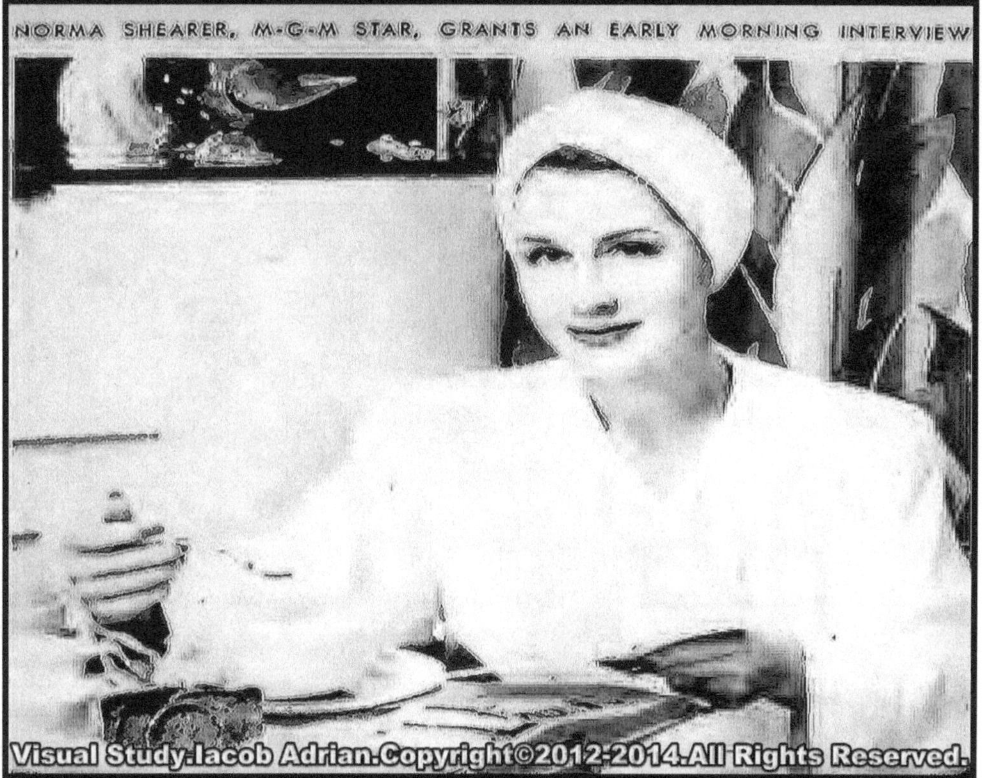

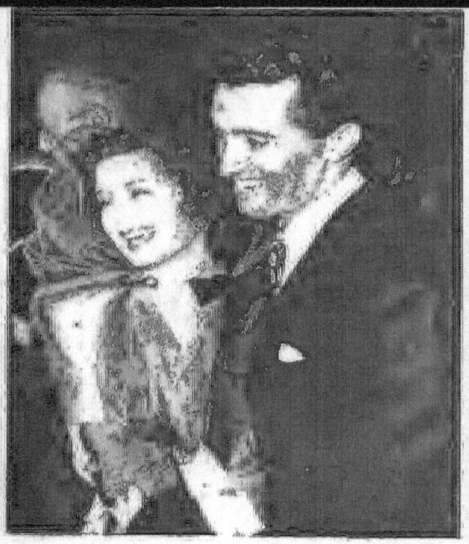

A beaming couple were Norma Shearer
and husband, Martin Arrouge, at the
reception f o l l o w i n g the Reginald
Gardiner-Nadia Petrova n u p t i a l s

Bibliographic sources :

Hollywood (1934-1943)
Publisher: Hollywood Magazine, inc. ; Fawcett Publications, inc.

The New Movie Magazine (1929-1935)
Publisher: Tower Magazines, inc.

This documentary study use,
combined in various proportions,
elements from the following categories,
forms and subsets :
- fair use
- documentary
- documentary photography
- feature
- journalism
- arts journalism
- visual journalism
- photojournalism
- celebrity photography
in order to :
- employ material as the object of cultural critique ,
- quote to illustrate an argument or point ,
- use material in historical sequence,
providing independent opinion,
using photos, press articles, advertisements,
opinions of fans etc. ...